TALES FROM THE

FROM THE

CADDIE MASTER

PALMETTO
PUBLISHING
Charleston, SC
www.PalmettoPublishing.com

Hardcover ISBN: 9798822957930
Paperback ISBN: 9798822957947
eBook ISBN: 9798822957954

TALES FROM THE CADDIE MASTER

Joe Schmerbeck

CONTENTS

ℙREFACE

The Caddie Master of Oak Hill Country Club in Rochester, New York, from 2003–2014 has written this document for the mere purpose of educating the general populace on the composition of a particular caddie program at an upscale, prestigious, historical, and private country club. The examples mentioned of caddies, golfers, members, guests, and situations may be representative of other golf and country clubs, be they private, semiprivate, or public. Private refers to those clubs usually owned and operated by their membership—generally the upper echelon of the corporate and social ladders (white-collar)—and, most likely, at a substantial cost. Semiprivate and public clubs target the less fortunate (blue-collar). Municipal (public) courses, in most cases, come under the jurisdiction of the local government, operated by the respective county.

There is a multitude of individuals I have taken the privilege, opportunity, and time to mention in this book, being somewhat mostly positive, but unfortunately, there are some negative aspects or situations I felt deserved some press. These characters included caddies, of course, but also head golf professionals, members, guests, professional athletes, coaches, comedians, musicians, other fellow employees, and so forth. The names have been changed in most cases to protect the innocent and the Caddie Master; others are considered well-known, and therefore no aliases were necessary.

It is a fact that I, together with my five siblings, were raised in an environment where honesty was virtuous. Back in those days, many years ago, that was the norm. Unfortunately, in today's irrespective world, it is the exception. The prime example these days is the media, hands down. No other faction of society even comes close, excluding the government. Enough said. The reason for mentioning honesty is to assure you, the reader, that I have been straightforward and truthful in all that I have written.

The Caddie Master strongly believes that some individuals will interpret several sections as being quite controversial; others may view it as highly self-opinionated, sarcastic, grossly exaggerated, politically motivated, perhaps a tad cocky, or whatever. If anyone concludes that the material seems fabricated (or one believes so) here or there, so be it. To quote an infamous historical figure: "What I have written, I have written" (John 19:22 NIV).

One may not perceive a story as fact, but when anyone mentioned something to yours truly, I believed and trusted that the information given to me by that individual was truthful and honest. Why would I not? At my age, I can logically conclude when someone was doing otherwise.

CADDIE: THE WORD'S ORIGIN AND APPLICATIONS

Before delving into this book, it is necessary to understand the use, variations, and applications of the word "caddie." From where did the word originate? Following proper research, we discover that the term originated in the vocabulary of Mary Queen of Scots, from the mid-sixteenth century. There are several different versions of Mary's use of the word "caddie." The noun is derived from the French *le cadet*, which, when translated, means "the boy." Some sources state that this term came into use when French prisoners of war were taken to Scotland after some historic battle. Other versions proclaimed that Mary Queen of Scots visited France to introduce the French hierarchy to the sport of golf. The sole purpose of these "caddies" was to carry the equipment of their masters. In the game of golf, this translated to carrying of the golf clubs and accessories. At that time in history, golf bags were nonexistent. So the caddie would bundle the equipment and proceed.

"Caddy" eventually became the American bastardization of a fine English noun. In the contents of this publication, "caddie" and "forecaddie" are nouns, whereas "caddy" and "forecaddy" are designated as verbs. The term "caddie master" refers to anyone who is in a supervisory position over caddies. And Caddie Master—capital *C* and capital *M*—refers solely to the author.

THE EARLY YEARS

Introduction

I acquired an interest for the game of golf at the ripe old age of fourteen. Due to my financial status at that time, I was limited to playing golf at the local "munies" (short for municipals), that is, the public golf courses operated by the county. At the age of fifteen, I added caddying at Oak Hill Country Club to my daily agenda after the school year finished. With the monies I received delivering the local morning newspaper (known as the *Democrat and Chronicle* in Rochester, NY) and caddying at Oak Hill Country Club (CC), I managed to pay my tuition at a local Jesuit high school, the institution I had chosen to attend.

In the Beginning

When I arrived at Oak Hill CC in early June of 1967, the caddie program was just getting underway for the summer, and being new at the caddie position, I was required to participate in the caddie training classes. At that time, there were perhaps sixty caddies on the roster since only members who were physically challenged and had their doctor's permission were allowed to traverse the golf course in a gas cart while they played their round of golf. All other members would have to walk the golf course; they had the choice of carrying their golf bag, pushing or pulling a personal cart, or employing a caddie.

Most of the male members and guests preferred to have a caddie carrying one or two bags, while a minority carried their "Sunday bags," which are very light and small, usually with just one small pocket for tees and a limited number of golf balls.

Back in those days, not many women played golf, but those who did usually had a personal cart they would push or pull along. The only time I remember caddying for a woman occurred early in my caddying days; I was assigned to carry Mrs. M's bag. The only problem there was Mrs. M did not have a golf bag but a personal cart with fourteen individual slots, one for every golf club. Not only was it awkward and embarrassing pushing a cart (I would label it slave-like labor), but it also limited where I could walk. Obviously, it is much easier to carry a bag or two across a tee or a green than push or pull a cart around these areas.

Reasons for Caddying

The reason why I, along with other teenagers, older boys and men, decided to be a caddie was, obviously, because the pay was excellent compared to other jobs at that age; plus, we could play unlimited golf on Mondays either on the East (Championship) Course or the West Course. On several occasions, I played fifty-four holes, twice on one course and once on the other.

The average rate for caddying at that time was four dollars per bag, plus the suggested tip of one Washington ($1), though the rate varied due to the nature of the golfer and the performance of the caddie, just to mention a couple of factors. A good A-rated caddie would average around seven dollars per bag.

Back in the day, the caddie classifications at Oak Hill CC were A, B, and C. If you succeeded in advancing into the established caddie program, you started as a C caddie and hopefully would eventually graduate through the ranks. It took me about a month to proceed to the B level and perhaps six more weeks to eventually reach the A status. The classification system will be explained in full detail later in this book.

I became an excellent caddie, and on many occasions, I was able to select the members for whom I wished to caddy, thanks to MC, who was the manager of the Golf Service Center at that time. For some odd reason, MC befriended me, treated me like a son, and favored me, unlike any other caddie.

The Brothers

I enjoyed all the members for whom I caddied; I don't remember ever having a bad or negative experience, except that one time with Mrs. M, as was previously mentioned. But there were two brothers who treated me quite well: Juan and Willie. (These are obviously aliases, since such names would define them as minorities, which were not allowed at Oak Hill CC or at most private clubs in the area, as well as in the rest of the country as a whole. Segregation and discrimination were the norms at this time in the history of the United States.) Both were low-handicap (good) golfers and extremely generous. Juan spent a portion of his career as a radio broadcaster on a local Top 40 AM channel, and together with Willie, they were well established in the restaurant and entertainment business, and perhaps other fields of which I was not aware. At that time, in the late 1960s, they owned and operated the largest nightclub in Monroe County.

When caddying for these two fine gentlemen, I was instructed to carry their leather Kangaroo golf bags down the middle of the fairway after they had struck their drives from the first tee, regardless of where the golf balls had landed. After studying the situation, each one would walk toward the caddie to select a club or two and return to their position for the next shot. This made the job somewhat easier. However, the golf bags weighed a ton, and I was still responsible for my other caddie duties, such as giving distances (there were no yardage devices in those days outside of painted stakes and the tops of sprinkler heads), raking traps, replacing divots, attending the flag, and reading putts (the path the golf ball would take to get to its destination based on such factors such as the "speed" of the green, the topography of the putting surface, type of grass, the grain, wind and so on). This continued for all eighteen holes.

As for their generosity, Juan and Willie always graded the caddie "Excellent" and paid twenty-five dollars. That made the round extremely worthwhile. Plus, once in a while, one of the brothers (usually Willie) would grant a perk—free admission to their nightclub (through the back door, of course, as my fellow caddie, KB, and I were underage). And so was life…

The Head Pro

Jack Lumpkin was the head golf professional when I caddied at Oak Hill CC in my earlier years. In those days, I caddied for the pro on multiple occasions, including several Western New York Professional Golfers Association events. Not only was Mr. Lumpkin munificent in his payment for my services, but also on several occasions when returning to the country club, he would make certain that I was properly fed. It was from these lunches that I learned to always cut one's sandwich in half. With eight mouths to feed in my family, and on a limited budget, going out for lunch or dinner was a once-in-a-year celebration.

There were many instances when Jack preferred to use the area located between the fourteenth and eighteenth holes on the East Course as his private practice ground. As a result, whoever was assigned to him would "shag" balls (that is, retrieve the golf balls with a mid-size leather zipper bag that hold just over 100 golf balls) in this space since it was outside the designated practice area. Other experiences caddying for Mr. Lumpkin will be mentioned shortly.

The US Open Championship 1968—The Draw

As many are aware, Oak Hill CC served as the host of the 1968 US Open Championship. Unlike today, contestants in the four majors (the Masters, the US Open, the British Open, and the PGA Championship) could not employ their personal caddies. As a result, the tournament directors researched for the best candidates to fill these positions. About three hundred caddies were selected from hundreds of résumés, and that list was narrowed to the final 170: 150 golfers and 20 extra caddies to serve as alternates in case a player was not satisfied with the caddie assigned to him. I was chosen as a finalist.

The names of the selected 170 caddies were put into one container and numbers from 1 to 170 in another. The caddies who drew numbers 1–150 would be matched with the player with the corresponding number; those who drew numbers 151–170 would serve as alternates (unfortunately).

I was the twentieth person called to draw a number. At that time, eleven alternative numbers had already been drawn, and only eight actual tournament caddies. So my odds were 142 to 9 that I would pick a winning number. I figured the odds of caddying in the 1968 US Open were greatly in my favor. So I proceeded to draw number 165! Shocking, devastating, unbelievable! Are you kidding me? To this day, the only things I have remaining from the 1968 US Open Championship are many memories and one lousy button that reads "1968 US Open Championship Caddie #165."

Figure 1: Caddie Button

The 1968 US Open Championship—Life after the Draw

MC, as I had mentioned before, was the Golf Service Center manager. He really felt sorry for me, but being left without a loop for the US Open did yield several other opportunities for me. When there is a major golf championship anywhere, both professional and amateur golfers alike begin practicing at the golf course, perhaps six to eight weeks (and in some cases even earlier) before the tournament is actually scheduled. So in this period before the championship began at Oak Hill CC, I was assigned to caddy various practice rounds for participating contestants, such as Dave Marr (about the nicest guy anyone would ever want to meet), Labron Harris Jr., Rocky Thompson, and Bert Yancey, just to name a few. Mr. Yancey referred to me as "the Bull." I really couldn't figure that one out since at the time, I stood about five foot five and tipped the scales at about a buck fifteen. I enjoyed caddying for all of them.

But the biggest moment in my caddie career occurred when I was assigned to caddie for Jack W. Lumpkin. Not that I hadn't caddied for the "Georgia Peach" before, but rounding out the foursome would be Arnold Palmer, Jack Nicklaus, and Tom Weiskopf! This was the greatest personal caddie memory that just cannot be forgotten.

About one half hour after the completion of the round when the other caddies had departed, MC approached me and inquired if

I would like to shag balls for Jack—not Lumpkin, but the "Golden Bear," Jack Nicklaus, himself! What an honor!

Now Mr. Nicklaus started with a sand wedge and directed me to the location where he wanted me to shag the golf balls (MacGregor's balls with the imprint of the Golden Bear on each one). After one bounce, I would catch the ball in my towel as he practiced with every club from sand wedge to the driver. Obviously, the longer the club, the more distance I would allow it to roll before retrieving it. I would dare to say that 90 percent of the golf balls he struck were right in front of me, making retrieving the golf balls quite an easy chore. He did manage to fly a couple of drives over my head, but the overall precision was phenomenal. When we had completed the practice, Mr. Nicklaus presented me with a firm handshake, a "thank you," and a ten-dollar bill, which was extremely generous at that time in history.

In another instance, MC requested me personally from the caddie yard to caddy for a contestant in the US Open for a practice round. He mentioned that the player was running a little late, but that I should be ready and prepared when he arrived. I proceeded to retrieve the golf bag from the player's automobile. This "player" had a first name of Gary, as in Gary Player. At that time, he was a member of the last triumvirate, along with Palmer and Nicklaus. After a few warm-up swings on the practice range, we started conversing on our way to the first tee of the East Course. Having arrived at the tee, I handed Mr. Player his driver as requested when, as fate would have it, his assigned caddie for the championship decided to make a late appearance. Unfortunately, it became another "good walk spoiled," to borrow a phrase from author John Feinstein.

Other Duties at the 1968 US Open

When I wasn't caddying, I was responsible for retrieving the contestants' golf bags at the designated bag drop area, where the players' left golf equipment upon arrival at the golf service center. I fondly remember taking care of Mr. Arnold Palmer. He dropped off his golf clubs there and requested I carry his duffel bag to his locker. After the task was completed, he handed me a "Lincoln," as in a five-dollar bill. In 1968, this was a very generous tip, considering that was what most caddies received for carrying a golf bag for eighteen holes, including a tip.

On another occasion, there was a gold Cadillac DeVille that arrived at the main entrance of the Oak Hill clubhouse. I approached the automobile in a Club Car (the name of the golf cart manufacturer) to retrieve the golfer's bag. The trunk opened, and I made an attempt to lift the bag onto my gasoline-powered golf cart. Before I could say "Doug Sanders," his chauffeur left the driver's seat and said, "Don't even try it. Let me help you." He grabbed the bottom of the bag while I positioned my arms around the upper part of the travel bag. For those who are not familiar with Mr. Sanders, he was the most flamboyant dresser on the tour. Between the golf bag and the outer traveling bag, about a dozen pairs of different colored golf shoes (with metal spikes) were lined up to be matched with the many colorful outfits hanging from a bar stretching from one side of the interior of the automobile to the other. Needless to say, the bag weighed a ton! We carried it as many others would have handled a corpse.

As for the remainder of the 1968 US Open, I fell two places short of actually caddying in the championship itself; alternate caddies went as far as number 163. Although I did not get an official loop in the US Open, I did have my share of wonderful experiences.

Lee Trevino's Stay during the US Open

During my tenure as Caddie Master at Oak Hill CC, one of my caddies informed me that Lee Trevino actually stayed at his grandfather's house when he was competing in the 1968 US Open Championship. This caddie came from a family whose name is synonymous with golf in the Greater Rochester area. Anyway, the story goes that late on Saturday night after the third round, June 15, 1968, Lee Trevino decided it was time for a couple cervezas at the nearby watering hole. Mind you, he was only one stroke off the lead going into the final round of the US Open! Supposedly, he arrived in Rochester with only a twenty-dollar bill in his pocket. Beers were much cheaper in those days than today, so he could have probably obtained one hell of a buzz on with twenty dollars. After others in the house convinced him that it would not be in his best interests and to call it a night, reluctantly he agreed, and the rest is history. Although virtually an unknown at that time, Trevino was picked in the top five to win the tournament. And at the conclusion of this event, he was crowned the winner of the 1968 US Open, his first of six Major championships in his brilliant career.

Oak Hill Country Club—Before and After

When I was employed there from 2002 until my retirement in 2014, Oak Hill CC in Rochester, NY, was always rated in the top thirty private country clubs in the United States, according to *Golf Digest*. In the October 2010 issue of *Golf World*, it was distinguished as the number one private country club in the nation for overall value, as voted by over sixty-five thousand golfers from across the country.

The questionnaire consisted of ten categories. They were

- quality of the course;
- course condition;
- reputation/prestige;
- practice facilities;
- speed of play;
- clubhouse/locker room;
- the caddie program, which had jumped from being rated number thirty in the last survey to number six, the largest percentage improvement of all ten categories;
- food quality;
- dining facilities; and
- overall value, based on all the amenities offered by the club that make the facility an enjoyable and memorable experience.

Rounding out the top ten ranked country clubs in the survey in 2010 were

#2—Chechessee Creek Club (Okatie, South Carolina)

#3—Augusta National Golf Club (Augusta, Georgia)

#4—Inverness Club (Toledo, Ohio)

#5—Kinloch Golf Club (Manakin-Sabot, Virginia)

#6—Hidden Creek Golf Club (Egg Harbor Township, New Jersey)

#7—Pine Valley Golf Club (Pine Valley, New Jersey)

#8—Robert Trent Jones Golf Club (Gainesville, Virginia)

#9—Oakmont Country Club (Oakmont, Pennsylvania)

#10—Cypress Point Club (Pebble Beach, California)

That is quite an array of the finest country clubs in the United States. Of course, in my opinion, Oak Hill CC would not have been where it was rated had history, tradition, and prestige (with a head pro named Harmon) not been considered in the evaluation, especially in the rankings of *Golf Digest*'s Top 100. There was also some speculation that the ballot boxes were stuffed! At Oak Hill? Could this possibly be true?

The Golf Course

Designed by a world-renowned golf architect, Donald Ross, the East and West, (the East being the Champion Course), has been the site of many golf tournaments, including the 1949 and 1998 US Amateur Championship; the 1956, 1968, and 1989 US Open; the 1980, 2003, 2013 and the 2023 Professional Golfers' Association Championship; the 1984 Seniors US Open Championship; the 2008 and 2019 Senior PGA Championship, and who can't forget the 1995 Ryder Cup.

Figure 2: Flag from all men's majors hosted by Oak Hill Country Club as mentioned above.

Head Professionals at Oak Hill (Pre-2014)

During my years at Oak Hill CC, I had the privilege to work for the head professionals Mr. Jack Lumpkin (as a caddie and bag room assistant) and Mr. Craig Wood Harmon in 2002 as an assistant manager in the Golf Service Center (GSC) and the remainder of my career at Oak Hill (2003–2014) as the Caddie Master. Both head professionals were outstanding gentlemen and a tribute to Oak Hill CC, as rated in *Golf Digest*'s Top 50 teaching professionals in the country.

Jack Lumpkin left Oak Hill CC in 1972, and Craig Harmon became the head golf professional. Mr. Harmon would remain there for forty-two seasons until his retirement at the end of the 2013 season, which was the year of a Major at Oak Hill CC, the 2013 PGA Championship won by Jason Dufner. Upon his retirement from Oak Hill CC, Craig Harmon eventually proceeded to become the director of golf at the Seagate Resort in Delray Beach, Florida, for a few years before returning as the teaching professional (at the time of the writing of this book) at Nick Price's MacArthur Park in Hobe Sound, Florida.

Craig Harmon

When I accepted the position as assistant manager of the Golf Service Center in 2002, I immediately became a member of Craig Harmon's professional staff. For those not familiar with the infamous Harmon family, there were four sons of the 1948 Masters champion, Claude Harmon. The four sons, well known in the golfing world, were named Butch, Craig, Dick, and Billy. Dick, sadly, passed away in 2006, but the other three sons are included as the most successful teachers in *Golf Digest*'s Top 50 instructors.

Butch is the most popular of the Harmon boys, especially for being the coach (for some time) of arguably one of the greatest golfers of all time, Tiger Woods. Also included in his list of students (past and present), you will find Phil Mickelson, Ernie Els, Seve Ballesteros, Nick Faldo, Fred Couples, Adam Scott, and others.

Craig Harmon, the second oldest, became the head golf professional at Oak Hill CC in 1972, replacing Jack Lumpkin, who relocated to Sea Island, Georgia. Unfortunately, Mr. Lumpkin passed away in early 2022 at the age of eighty-six. He was one of the greatest instructors in golf history. During the winter months, one could locate Craig at MacArthur Park in Hobe Sound, Florida.

The Latter Years

Employment at Oak Hill Country Club 2002–2014

On June 13, 2003, I was approached by the manager of the Golf Service Center, Mr. Dyxmit, who inquired if I was interested in becoming the Caddie Master, since the position had become available. But how did I get there? I caddied there as a teenager, possessed a college degree, and was employed by a company known as Eastman Kodak for twenty-seven years. Due to the terrorist attack of September 11, 2001, the management of Kodak decided it was time to reorganize, which led to hundreds of layoffs, mostly workers over forty-five years of age who would be eligible for retirement (and pension) in the near future. (It was age discrimination, to say the least, comparable to the post-2013 era at Oak Hill CC.)

Being fed up and disgusted with the greed and unethical practices of corporate America, I applied to be assistant manager of the Golf Service Center in April of 2002. I was interviewed by Mr. Dyxmit and realized our backgrounds had many similarities, which resulted in a lengthy and excellent conversation.

I later discovered that Mr. Dyxmit preferred applicants who approached a job interview the "old-fashioned" way—dress slacks, shirt and tie, sport coat, and overall neat appearance, the professional look as should be expected at a country club of this stature. Obviously, my appearance at the interview met his expectations.

In our conversation, I was startled to learn that some of the individuals I had caddied for in my adolescent years were still members at Oak Hill CC. In the end, Mr. Dyxmit offered me the position as an assistant manager of the Golf Service Center. Mr. Dyxmit was extremely well organized and ran a tight ship. He was highly respected by everyone—fellow workers, management, Craig Harmon, members, caddies, the press, as well as celebrities and sports figures who teed it up at Oak Hill CC. With these celebrities and professionals, Mr. Dyxmit would approach these individuals upon their arrival or after the conclusion of their round to add their signature to "The Wall ."

The Wall was located on the inside of the Golf Service Center, which would also be considered as the bag room or Mr. Dyxmit's office. On this wall, you would find the signatures of such people as Phil Mickelson (PG.A), Jim Kelly (NFL), Steve Tasker (NFL), Cal Ripken Jr. (MLB), Marv Levy (NFL), Mike Shanahan (NFL), Mark Rypien (NFL), Scotty Bowman (NHL), Tyler Ennis (NHL), Thurman Thomas (NFL), Jason Dufner (PGA), Bobby Nichols (PGA), Joe Amato (NHRA), "Doc" Rivers (NBA), Jim Craig (1980 Winter Olympics), Mike Eruzione (1980 Winter Olympics), Dean Smith (NCAA), Jay Wright (NCAA), Jim Boeheim (NCAA), Jay Bilas (NCAA), (Alonzo Mourning (NBA), Bobby Grich (MLB), Natalie Gulbis (LPGA), Cheyenne Woods (LPGA), Bob Thomas (NFL), Dave Merritt (NFL), Trevor Hoffman (MLB), Pete Mahovlich (NHL), Eddie Johnston (NHL), Brian Gionta (NHL), Clarke MacArthur (NHL), Greg Anthony (NBA), John Starks (NBA), Jeff Sluman (PGA), Joey Sindelar (PGA), Ron White (a comedian—how did he get in here?), and dozens of others.

Transition from GSC to Caddie Master

In the spring of 2003, an issue arose concerning the cashing of the caddies' chits. It so happened that a good number of bogus chits had been dispensed by the Golf Service Center managers. We were informed by the accounting department that a member had discovered discrepancies in his account for the month of May. It wasn't a surprise to him to have caddie fees; the only problem was that he was seeing a charge from a particular caddie for services rendered on dates while he had been on a business trip in Boston! The managers were able to trace the evidence back to a relative of the caddie master. The caddie had memorized the member's account number and therefore proceeded to falsify several chits with said account number and a forged signature. The general manager of Oak Hill CC then scheduled a meeting including himself, Mr. Dyxmit, yours truly, the other assistant manager, and the caddie master to discuss in detail the circumstances. Even though all assortments of incriminating evidence were presented, the caddie master denied having any knowledge of the situation. He even went as far as saying that his relative was innocent and that we, the managers of the Golf Service Center, were guilty of fabrication! Mr. Dyxmit was livid! I had never experienced him being so angry. He used words I had never heard him say or repeat! It was my belief that an altercation was inevitable. The general manager whisked the caddie master away from the conference room. In the meantime, Mr. Dyxmit, with some assistance, was seated and composed himself.

About a week had passed when Mr. Dyxmit invited me to his office, along with the other assistant manager, to discuss the newly vacant caddie master position. Since I had caddied at Oak Hill in my adolescent years, was familiar with the caddie program, and had even caddied for several members in the past, I graciously accepted the position as the Caddie Master. And that, my dear readers, was how it all began. Even though it was strongly suggested that the previous caddie master be terminated from working at Oak Hill, the board of directors stated that this individual could retain his status as an honor caddie at the club since many of the board members and others were well aware of his caddying expertise and believed that firing him would be excessive.

Winters in Florida

During my time as the Caddie Master at Oak Hill CC, I would spend my winters in Stuart, Florida, where I usually resided from mid-October until the beginning of the golf season in early April in the Northeast.

The warm and beautiful weather in the southeastern United States would be replaced by snow, rain, wind, and the raw conditions of upstate New York. I, like many of the snowbirds, emphatically dreaded this time of the year. Whether I arrived in New York from the southern or western part of the state, my wife and I would be greeted by a white covering on the earth. I believe it was April of 2013 when more than a foot of snow was observed at a "Welcome to New York" road sign via Erie, Pennsylvania. While in Florida, I was employed at a couple of private country clubs: the Turtle Creek Club in Tequesta and the Tesoro Country Club in Palm City. The Tesoro Club was the brainchild of Bobby Ginn (CEO of the Ginn Corporation, a real estate development company) and boasted two golf courses, one designed by Arnold Palmer and the other by Tom Watson. A new clubhouse was being constructed in the style of Spanish architecture at a cost of fifty million dollars (plus or minus a couple million). Before it was completed, the Tesoro Club filed for bankruptcy. That occurred in 2008 at the height of the recession.

Since I was employed in Florida, I stated on the Oak Hill CC web page that I would not be accepting any applications for the caddie training program until April 15th, regardless of the year. Unfortunately, either people cannot read or they think it does not apply to them. Requests for employment prior to April 15th resulted in a deletion from my email inbox.

We decided to relocate and become Florida residents (thanks mostly to taxes, the teachers' union, the politics, etc. of New York State), and to purchase a home to enjoy the winters, not for me to be concerned about training candidates for the upcoming golf season.

Returning to Begin Another Season

As I stated earlier, I really dreaded going back in April to the cold dampness of Upstate New York. The first thing on the agenda when I returned to Oak Hill CC was to prepare the caddie area. That meant raking leaves, sweeping, arranging the outdoor furniture, hanging up billboards, posting the current caddie roster, and having conversations with various other employees. This would include the manager of the Golf Service Center, the general manager of Oak Hill CC, and, of course, Craig Harmon. The purpose of these chats was to be informed of changes at the club, new members, and possible adjustments in policies and procedures. Also included would be any changes in the events for the year, such as corporate outings, men's and women's tournaments, and other outside activities.

For the most part, the annual outings and tournaments occurred during the same week as the previous year or years. During my time there at Oak Hill CC, there were three Majors hosted by the club: the 2003 and 2013 PGA Championships and the 2008 Senior PGA Championship. The PGA Championship was also scheduled to finish on the second Sunday of August, which meant that the Men's Invitational had to be rescheduled to another date. The Senior PGA Championship was to be held the week before Memorial Day, when, at that time, no member tournaments were scheduled. I recall that for most of the days in that tournament, the low temperatures were in the mid-forties and the highs in the sixties—"cool" for a Major championship.

After all this preliminary preparation for the upcoming season was completed, I began to lay the groundwork for the caddie training sessions. These informational meetings usually took place on the first three Mondays of May, followed by the Western PGA Caddie Test on the following Monday or Tuesday, depending on the holiday. Those who succeeded to advance into the caddie program would be able to start on or around on June 1st. Unfortunately, due to the number of veteran caddies returning, usually only three to six candidates prevailed in any given year.

After I was appointed Caddie Master in June of 2003 (before I trained any caddies), I had a reasonable idea of what I needed to accomplish and set my goals to be one of the premier caddie programs in the country. The closest country club that had any resemblance of a good, solid caddie program was the Country Club of Buffalo (CCB), about seventy miles from Oak Hill CC.

I phoned the caddie master at the CCB to make an arrangement to spend a day at his club. Now this gentleman was not only the caddie master but also supervisor of the cart barn, the practice facility, starter, and ranger. But for the most part, we talked and discussed caddies, different behaviors, caddie rules and regulations, and rates.

In my rookie year as Caddie Master, the caddie rates at Oak Hill CC were something like twenty-five dollars plus tip for an honor caddie; twenty dollars plus tip for an A caddie, and eighteen dollars plus tip for B, or the least experienced and skillful of the three classifications. For a place like Oak Hill CC, I felt these rates were relatively low, but they were even lower at CCB! I remember back in 2003 when the rates at many private country clubs were in the $50–$60 range plus tip and, in several cases, even higher. I will further discuss this topic later in this book.

When I first started training caddies in 2004, I would not accept any candidates younger than fourteen years of age. That lasted exactly one year. I learned in that short period that children this age were too young and immature to fit into my plan of constructing a successful caddie program for a country club with the stature and prestige of Oak Hill CC.

I particularly remember one instance when I was observing two fourteen-year-old caddies attempting to acquire a position on the caddie roster. One was 5′10″, and his friend was barely five feet in height. I had assigned them (and two other seasoned caddies) to Mr. I and his three guests. Upon the completion of the round, I requested the member rate the caddies on their performance. He stated that the taller lad (whose father happened to be a retired professional hockey player, which I was not aware of at the time) had a very good performance, as the guest also had mentioned. The member had insisted on the smaller lad caddying for him. I believed the member figured this new caddie might not survive until the end of the round (all eighteen holes), and none of his guests would tote their own golf bag. He explained to me that the caddie was a good kid but only lasted fourteen holes due to his physical limitations. In the end, the decision was logical. Based on skills and performance, I selected the taller boy for the caddie program but reluctantly dismissed his shorter friend.

The following week, I was approached by the father of the young lad I had dismissed. After I shared the reason for his son's dismissal, he stared at me and said, "Do you know who I am?"

"No, sir, I do not know who you are," I replied. Nor did I care; I didn't need to be pressured by someone I couldn't identify. It happened that this gentleman was a relatively new sportscaster for a local television station. I did not know or recognize the individual because I faithfully watched the news, sports, and weather on a different channel. So this is just another example of what the Caddie Master must go through in an attempt to have a quality caddie program.

Let it be known that this applicant (or anyone who was not accepted that year) could have re-applied to become a caddie in any of the following seasons, but he never took advantage of the opportunity.

The Caddie Situation in 2003

As I had stated earlier, I was given the position of Caddie Master in 2003; I inherited a somewhat loosely organized program of about thirty caddies, close to half of which were members' offspring despite a statute in the Oak Hill CC Gold Book stating that a member's children could not be employed by Oak Hill CC. It was never enforced; for whatever reason, it was, more or less, ignored.

It appeared the manner in which this was interpreted by caddies who were children of the members was that they could not be directly employed by the club because caddies are considered independent contractors and therefore are not employed directly by Oak Hill CC. It was my belief that was not the original intention when the rules and regulations were initially implemented.

I proceeded to schedule a meeting with the general manager to discuss this situation. It was then decided by the GM and the board of directors that I would no longer select members' children to be caddies at Oak Hill CC; on the other hand, I had to grandfather in those members' children who were presently part of the official caddie program.

The Training

The actual training of new candidates consisted of learning materials provided by the Western Golf Association (WGA), known for the Evans Scholarship in Chicago, Illinois.

The main source of the training session was a video supplied by the WGA on becoming a good caddie. For the most part, it was an excellent presentation, but there were a few segments where I disagreed.

My personal belief on a caddie carrying a stand bag was quite different than what was presented in the video. When a caddie offers the bag to the golfer for club selection, the video shows a caddie standing in the fairway where his player would be hitting his next shot. The bag stands on its two legs by itself, whereas the caddie stands there with his hands in his pockets, arms crossed, or whatever. This is just plain lazy. The caddie, I believe, should offer the bag to his player for selection by having the bag upright with his support instead of using the stand. If the clubs are offered without the aid of the caddie, there is more friction from the grips in the bottom of the bag from the golf clubs being too close together. Also, in most cases, the golfer must bend over to select his club of choice.

Let me give you a couple of examples. First of all, I observed a golf bag being blown over by a gust of wind while the caddie appeared to be daydreaming. In another instance, I warned a caddie twice not to leave the golf bag freestanding. Needless to say, a couple of days later, there he was with his arms crossed; I had to dismiss him. This policy applied to single caddies, who were responsible for only one golfer.

As part of my job, I would often drive around in a Club Car with my field glasses to spy on my caddies and their performances. It was a pleasure observing that some of the new caddies actually learned something during the training sessions. It was even more of a delight noticing the look on a returning caddie's face when I questioned him on why he was standing on the wrong side (in the line of the putt) of the hole on #8 while attending the flag!

After the training sessions and the test, I would have candidates caddy for one of my honor caddies, many of whom were low-handicap golfers. This would allow me to rate the caddies and observe if they measured up to my standards. I would also obtain written reports from the honor caddies on all the candidates in their respective foursomes.

There were two sessions of nine-holes, one at 4:00 p.m. and the other around 6:15 p.m. In this way, I was able to rate and rank the wannabe caddies. I know for a fact that I did not advance more than eight (usually three or four) new caddies in any given year.

After my first year, I decided to raise the minimum age from fourteen to sixteen years old. This way, I was able to obtain a more mature and physically capable group of boys to caddy at Oak Hill CC. Added to this would be a provision stating that future caddies must actually play golf and be familiar with the rules, regulations, and etiquette of the game. Even though the crop of new caddies definitely improved the caddie program year after year, it took me five more years before I was completely satisfied and extremely comfortable with my crew. This occurred when I was confident that I could assign any caddie with any member or guest, knowing that the loop would be more than satisfactory and thereby instilling in the Caddie Master a most pleasurable feeling of confidence.

B Classifications

Of all the country clubs of which I am familiar, all caddies are classified according to their skill levels. Many country clubs use the A, B and C system. This was true when I caddied at Oak Hill CC as a teenager. However, when I returned later in life as Caddie Master, the classifications had been changed to Honor, A, and B. I will explain the latter format, since that is the one that was in practice when I acquired the caddie program at Oak Hill.

I will begin at the bottom with the B classification and eventually advance to those caddies labeled as Honor. The B caddie has demonstrated throughout the training sessions a desire to become a good and dependable caddie. At this stage of the game, the B caddie would be familiar with the basics, namely, where to stand, how to calculate the distance to the middle of the green, (notice I did not mention to the flagstick), replace divots, rake the sand traps, and attend the flag. The B caddie starts off primarily as a bag carrier, but in my program, they will not remain so. If they are content solely as a bag carrier, they will not last.

The liaison to the caddie program (a member, Mr. C. A. R), once approached me and suggested, "Why don't you have just a few kids as bag carriers?" Just about every time this gentleman visited a country club that had a caddie program that did something different, he thought it would be beneficial to my program (all his suggestions were humbly denied). I responded that I trained and hired caddies; I did not employ "bag carriers." It was not fair to the caddie nor the golfers. I realized there were some golfers (a couple, perhaps) who would use bag carriers, mainly due to them being the lowest rated of all the caddies and therefore the cheapest. Obviously, the farther a caddie advances up the caddie ladder, the better they will be compensated for his/her services.

A Classification

Forward to the A caddie. To advance to this stage, a caddie only needs to be rated Excellent by his golfers on five consecutive occasions and different golfers to graduate from the B status. At the end of the round, the player receives a blank report card from the caddie to grade him on several different categories. The rating system works as follows: Excellent, Good, Fair, and Poor. The criteria on which the caddie is evaluated includes where they stood, replacing divots, attending the flag, giving distances, etiquette, behavior, appearance, interest in the game, and a few others. There were ten categories altogether.

The newly graduated A caddie would still be a little green in most cases but was constantly improving. The caddie, through more loops, was educating himself by observing what other seasoned caddies were doing during the round, as well as communicating with said caddies and the Caddie Master.

As I admitted earlier, on many occasions I would proceed to the cart barn to an empty Oak Hill CC Club Car with my trusty field glasses and spy on the less-experienced caddies and jot down notes on where they needed improvement. When the round had been completed, I would then take the lad aside and review what

I had observed. Not only did this benefit the individual, but it also assisted me in maintaining a quality caddie program.

At the A level, the caddie would notice that due to his improved status, he would be assigned more often to caddy than remaining in the caddie yard. Being scheduled to caddy more often usually meant the quality of the players would also improve, since many low-hand-icap and scratch golfers prefer caddies in lieu of riding carts.

Depending on the caddie himself, he may have waited anywhere from one or two months and up to a couple of years to attain an honor classification; it is totally up to his commitment and determination. A teenager who is younger (say sixteen or seventeen) and just started caddying and who played golf sparingly would not possess the same skills as another caddie who was a member of a high school or college golf team. The reason being is that the latter would have much more exposure to the game, and therefore many of the techniques used in caddying would seem just plain logical.

Usually, an A caddie would be coupled with an honor caddie for the purpose of enhancing his skills, thus being educated on advancing to the next tier. He would excel at the basics after caddying more rounds at the A level. Pushing himself to become a world-class caddie, he would learn to walk off yardages to measure distances (before the introduction of range finders, which most caddies would invest in later). It was also at this stage of his caddie career when he would become more of an assistant to the golfer, helping him or her in other ways, such as club selection, wind and elevation factors, and, probably most importantly, reading greens. The more loops at this level would enable the caddie to familiarize himself with the golfer's game since he would be caddying for the same players (usually per request) on many occasions.

Honor Classification

When finally graduating to the honor level, the caddie would have now achieved his goal. It was at this stage where requests, either by members or guests, outnumbered assignments and waiting in the caddie yard, so to speak. They have become one of the cream of the crop. Caddies who had acquired this status became more household names in the clubhouse, and therefore had their schedules filled with requests. When I was the Caddie Master, I probably possessed at least a dozen or more caddies at any given time who were requested by an assortment of many different golfers (mostly members). This occurred after six full seasons at the helm; that was the timeframe needed to create a successful caddie program where I was totally comfortable with all my selections.

Caddie Rules

There are many rules that are needed to operate a decent caddie program. According to the video and the caddie manual provided by the WGA, the three "ups" of caddying are "Show up, keep up, and shut up!" Now in this day and age, it still holds true for new caddies who are still learning the ropes. However, most golfers nowadays insist on someone to talk to and communicate with rather than someone just toting their golf bag. The more comfortable a player is with his caddie, *usually* the better his game and his overall disposition will be. For this reason, many golfers will request the same caddie or caddies just about every time. The only problem here is when the caddie master is limited in his quantity of excellent workers and the preferred caddie or caddies are involved with another loop, meaning there are no other caddies remaining of their caliber. Fortunately, I had enough excellent caddies in the program that it really never became an issue (with the exception of the 2013 Men's Invitational. I will further explain that situation later in this book).

So to continue with the caddie rules. Obviously, most would conclude that the regulations are quite logical—no fighting, no swearing, no horseplay, no stealing, obey the orders as given by the Caddie Master or any other supervisors of the club. Also included were no consumption of alcoholic beverages, no illicit drugs, and respect for all the other caddies, as well as anyone with whom the caddie may come in contact. Also, no belittling of anyone or dismissal would be imminent. Furthermore, if a caddie was assigned a tee time for any future date, they must be present in the caddie yard forty-five minutes prior to tee time. Refusal to caddy for anyone to whom a caddie had been assigned was a guaranteed reason for termination as a caddie at Oak Hill Country Club.

One issue that really disgusted the Caddie Master was the overall appearance of some of the caddies. Where do I begin? Hats on backward, untucked shirts without collars or wrinkled (usually both), untied and soiled sneakers, and facial piercings (including one tongue)! But the worst culprit were cargo pants and shorts. Totally unacceptable. These so-called stylish garments had no business at Oak Hill, none whatsoever. I took it upon myself to implement a dress code.

From that point forward, only khaki pants and shorts would be worn with a collared white shirt and a decent pair of sneakers. Oak Hill CC monogrammed hats and visors were available at discounted prices. All clothing and outerwear were the responsibility of the caddies. This dress code was the norm at most country clubs; some country clubs provided the caddies with their official outfit, but the majority did not.

Abuse of the Caddie Rules

There are several rules that were consistently being disregarded, and if I and other caddie masters truly enforced them, we would have possessed a very limited field to operate an effective caddie program. It was indeed a toss-up among some of the rules least followed, including the use of foul language, conversations about sexual exploits, alcohol and drug use, and missed assignments. It was my belief that these four categories ran neck and neck for most common, but I would give the nod to the use of foul language; it occurred every single day, without a doubt. It appeared to me that caddies, especially the millennials, could not mention any noun without inserting their favorite adjective, the f-bomb. I mean, seriously—there was one caddie who used f-bombs so frequently, he used them to describe other f-bombs! I was constantly scolding this college student for such unacceptable language. The problem here was that they didn't even realize they were swearing. What is swearing in today's world, anyway?

The Caddie Yard

Now the caddie yard at Oak Hill CC was a space, perhaps forty feet by fifteen feet, that was located between the Golf Service Center and the main road to the clubhouse. Between May and mid-October, this area was covered by a huge green tarp that was fastened to the main structure to protect the caddies and the Caddie Master from the elements. This road was heavily traveled by pedestrians (mainly members coming from the parking area), either to access the locker room and the fitness center (a secondary entrance) or proceed to the main entrance, which included the dining areas, the museum (a must-see for guests), the ballroom, and, of course, the grill room. Although the caddie area was somewhat covered, sound traveled easily. There were no barriers to prevent this. There was perhaps ten feet of landscaping separating the caddie area from the roadway, but this was cosmetic at best. So if the caddies were not going to monitor their conversations, the Caddie Master would. Unfortunately, this would not be an easy task.

Figure 3: Renovation of the caddie yard (2012).

Since the caddie area was so limited, there was room for no more than two picnic tables and one smaller hexagonal table not more than three feet across. This piece of furniture served as my office desk. Voices and other assorted noises flowed freely from this area. A solid brick or cement wall would have been the best solution for this tiny space of real estate. The majority of the caddies on my roster in any given year were between the ages of sixteen and twenty-four. Payment for caddying in this age group was extremely high, so purchasing alcoholic beverages was not a problem for most caddies, especially since fake IDs, as everyone was aware, were so rampant.

So, with the availability of alcohol (and illegal drugs, let's not forget) came missed assignments. Luckily, if this occurred in the summertime, I always had other caddies available in the caddie yard. There were always caddies to act as backups in these situations. One instance cannot escape my memory.

There was a member at Oak Hill CC who also possessed membership at Valhalla CC, in Louisville, KY), North Shore CC in Chicago, IL, Willoughby CC in Stuart, FL, and, I believe, perhaps a few other private country clubs. Mr. W. S. was the owner of an oil and gas company in Louisville and always adhered to a strict schedule. He would arrive in Rochester, New York, aboard his private jet with his guests, who would accompany him from other metropolises, sometimes landing in their respective airports for their convenience. His arrival at Oak Hill CC would be at 7:30 a.m. sharp, and he would then proceed to the locker room before breakfast in the Oak Room. At 8:45 a.m., his foursome would be ready to move onward to the driving range to warm up while Mr. W. S. diverted to the caddie area to discuss the caddie situation with the Caddie Master.

Mr. W. S. always requested two honor double caddies. On this one particular day, I assigned to his group two honor caddies, one being JD. Now JD always had a tendency to be a little late, no matter what. Since Mr. W. S.'s tee time was always 9:30 a.m., I vehemently reminded the lad to be there on time! He always played the East Course and paid his caddies well, so why would JD—or any caddie, for that matter—risk not being on time? As previously mentioned, caddies knew they must be signed in at least forty-five minutes prior to the scheduled tee time. On this particular day at 8:45 a.m., JD was nowhere in sight. So I assigned TW to carry two bags and, together with the other honor caddie, they followed Mr. W. S. to the practice area.

As expected, JD appeared five minutes late and donned his caddie attire. I approached him and questioned him on what his intentions were. He answered that he was preparing to head over to the driving range to relieve TW of what he thought was TW's temporary assignment. Next, I questioned JD on what time he was supposed to be ready. He did remember 8:45 a.m., but now, unfortunately, that was ten minutes ago; he had forfeited his loop.

Caddie Observations

Caddies, in general, always believed they were included in the "Top Ten" of all caddies in any respective caddie program when it came to rating themselves. That was the reason behind the Caddie Master taking the responsibility of walking to the cart barn, obtaining a Club Car, and traveling around both the East and West Courses to observe personally how efficiently or inefficiently these caddies performed their duties. I would be armed with my Bushnell field glasses in order to remain hidden and would get feedback from the golfers themselves to receive even a better idea of where the caddies should be ranked.

I remember several occasions where caddies would inform me of just how great they were at their position. In one particular case, a caddie I will refer to as Jody returned to the caddie yard boasting of his precision in reading the greens. The only problem here would be that two minutes after his speech, the member, Mr. P., approached the Caddie Master and claimed that the caddie (a first-year caddie who happened to be a college professor) was a real gentleman and a good caddie, but he couldn't read a green to save his life! And it happens all the time in the caddie world—just because a caddie gives the player a line on where to putt or says something like "a ball and a half to the right of the cup" and the player proceeds to make the putt doesn't translate to the golfer's acceptance of the caddie's advice! If the caddie did possess the skill of reading the greens, the member, guest, or whoever the caddie was assisting usually made it a point to mention this aspect of the game to the caddie but always brought it to the attention of the Caddie Master.

Caddies—Geographic Location

Many people wonder how much money a caddie actually gets paid for carrying a bag or two or forecaddying. There are many factors involved. The first factor was one I had been told by a member on the board of directors at Oak Hill CC but I don't totally agree with, which was that one must look at the demographics of where the golf course (country club) was located. Was it in a small market or large market area? Obviously, a caddie in Rochester, New York, would not be paid the same as a caddie from a large metropolitan area such as New York, Chicago, Philadelphia, Los Angeles, and so on. (It is my belief that if a caddie is equal to or better than those found in country clubs *of the same caliber*, then they should be paid accordingly.) Also, one must observe the quality of the golf course, whether it is a private, semiprivate, or a public facility. Where does the course rank, locally, statewide, and nationally? Is the caddie program rated successfully, as well as the caddies themselves? Of course, there were other factors involved, but these were perhaps the most crucial.

Caddie Pay Rates and Report Cards

When I first became Caddie Master in June of 2003, I felt the caddie rates at Oak Hill CC were somewhat pathetic. If I remember correctly, the honor caddie received twenty-five dollars per bag plus tip (suggested gratuity at five to ten dollars per bag). The A caddie would be paid at the rate of twenty dollars per bag (suggested gratuity at five dollars), and, of course, the B caddie would earn a paltry eighteen dollars for the same role (plus the generous tip also suggested at five dollars per bag). These tips were only suggested and, on numerous occasions, were even less. B caddies were not permitted to carry double (that is, two bags at a time, one on each shoulder), due solely to their lack of experience. Forecaddie rates were not listed, probably due to the fact that even though it was written in the Oak Hill CC Gold Book, the rule was never enforced.

Now I need to restate that in the old days, when I caddied at the beloved country club starting in 1966, the rate was four dollars per bag plus a suggested tip of one dollar for an honor caddie. Do the math. A round of golf in those days lasted approximately four and a half hours on the average. So at five dollars a round (rate plus tip), the caddie was pocketing a buck plus change for carrying a bag over eighteen holes. In the end, the caddie had probably traversed seven to eight miles of real estate with, in the majority of cases, two bags on his shoulders!

Time for a Raise

Since day one, I have pushed for higher wages for my caddies. I approached "the Ruler," (the general manager of the club at that time) and suggested an increase in the caddie pay scale. He instructed the Caddie Master to compare the rates at Oak Hill CC with other private country clubs in that part of the northeastern section of the country with somewhat comparable populations. I was to differentiate the level of pay at these clubs versus Oak Hill CC. These private clubs included Inverness in Toledo, Ohio; the Kahkwa Club in Erie, Pennsylvania; and the Country Club of Buffalo. The rates at these clubs, believe it or not, were right in line with those at Oak Hill, plus or minus a buck or two. The Country Club of Buffalo was the worst, at a meager eighteen dollars per bag plus tip for an honor caddie. Now none of these clubs mentioned were even close to Oak Hill in relation to history, tradition, and prestige, but that had no bearing, according to the Ruler. To the Caddie Master, this study was flawed. The word "comparable" to the GM (and some members on the board) meant in size of the city, whereas I thought it should have been put on the same scale with clubs of similar qualities, such as Winged Foot, Oakmont, and perhaps Congressional or Medinah. Even an average of all the clubs mentioned would, in my opinion, have been a better indicator of an honest wage. So in essence, it took six years in my career as Caddie Master to acquire a five-dollar increase across the board for all classifications. Eventually, near the end of 2012 (my tenth year), I achieved in elevating the rates even higher to forty dollars per bag for my honor caddies, thirty-five dollars for an A, and thirty dollars for a B caddie. The new suggested gratuities went from five to ten dollars to ten to twenty dollars for the honor caddies and ten dollars per bag for the other two classifications. It was brought to my attention after I retired at the conclusion of the 2014 season that the rating system had been discontinued by the new regime and the golfers basically paid the caddie(s) what they felt was appropriate. Go figure.

Caddie Rates at Other Country Clubs

Let me state for a fact that I was well aware before my retirement at Oak Hill CC that caddies at many different country clubs and resorts around the US were making eighty to one hundred dollars per bag plus gratuity. This was especially true coming from the metropolises such as New York, Chicago, Miami, Los Angeles, and so forth.

For the most part, when I did have guests golfing at Oak Hill, they would tend to pay their caddies in the same manner in which they compensated their own caddies at their respective country clubs from these aforementioned areas. This translated in the vicinity of two to five hundred dollars per double caddie! This was most common for the golfers who came to play Oak Hill CC as unaccompanied guests—in other words, there were no members from the host club in the group, regardless of whether it was a onesome or a foursome. Unaccompanied guests on Oak Hill's famed East Course shelled out four hundred dollars for the opportunity to play eighteen holes, plus the financial responsibility of the caddies.

On the other hand, if a member had invited three guests (forecaddie required if they were not employing bag-carrying caddies) and they paid for the services, the caddie would receive substantially less for their workmanship, as opposed to a single or double. On top of that, on many occasions when a guest would offer the caddie a tip after a member had settled with the caddie(s) financially, the member would intervene to inform the guest that no more gratuities were necessary. What a letdown for the caddie! Was the payer frugal or cheap? I know for a fact it was the latter. What really rattled me was who were they to tell someone else how to spend their money when coming to this venue or anywhere else?

How (and How Not) to Pay a Caddie

The following are some basic insights on the payment of a caddie. First of all, if you possess little or no idea and there are no guidelines available for fulfilling your obligation of compensating the person responsible for lugging your bag (or bags) around the course or a forecaddie, *always* ask the Caddie Master! Most of the time, the member—or guest, in some cases—will submit a chit informing the Caddie Master what he wishes to pay the caddie and have that amount charged to their personal account at Oak Hill or, if it was indeed a kind gesture of the guest's, the amount would be entered on their account at their respective country club. The caddie master, in most cases, has access to the club's bank account and can pay the caddies' wages according to the figure written on the chit and charged to the member's or guest's personal account at their respective country club.   Therefore, the caddie master has the best knowledge of what his caddies are being paid for their services and can inform the golfer of an amount that would be appropriate.

Be aware that there are dishonest caddie masters. Some caddie masters require kickbacks from the caddies, usually garnishing a percentage of their wages. I know of several caddie masters who have lost their positions due to this unethical labor practice. I also believe it to be more common than most people realize.

The greatest advice I can give any golfer who has the privilege of having a caddie is never, never, *never* ask the caddie directly what amount he should be paid. Many caddies believe they possess a seat in the upper echelon of the caddie program in regard to their skills. Obviously, they will give you a grossly inflated figure. If you are puzzled or confused (usually the chit or caddie report card will offer a guide of suggested rates plus tip), always consult the caddie master.

On the other hand, in regard to paying a caddie, refrain from asking an assistant pro or other employees (outside of the head professional, if he uses the caddie program—Jack Lumpkin and Craig Harmon were very faithful in using caddies). Caddies, for the most part, are independent contractors (though there are exceptions) and not Oak Hill Country Club employees. As such, they are paid much better than the assistant pros. So, in essence, these pros who are employed by the club may give you a somewhat lower dollar amount because of their jealousy. In fact, I had several assistant pros who eventually became part of the caddie program because the salary was significantly higher than being employed in the pro (or golf) shop. This practice was eventually discontinued by Craig Harmon.

Other Methods of Caddie Payment

As I had previously mentioned, there are some exceptions to caddies being independent contractors. In my early years as Caddie Master, I was contacted by a representative from Caddie Services Inc. (CSI), inquiring if I was interested in joining their company. When I questioned the gentleman on his reasoning for wanting me on their staff, he informed me that he heard I had created an excellent caddie program.

What my duties would involve would be to instruct other personnel on becoming caddie masters around the country, who would eventually build or maintain the existing caddie program. The caddies, therefore, would become employees of CSI and therefore would be paid by weekly check, minus taxes. My understanding (through conversations with a couple of caddies who worked for CSI in Florida during the winter months) was that the caddie would be paid a certain amount, depending on the golfers he caddied for in that period. The example given to me was a member (golfer) who wished for his caddie to receive $200. His account would be billed $240; $200 to the caddie and $40 to CSI.

Caddie Services Inc. is only one of many for-profit organizations around the country that train caddies and caddie masters. These were present at many prestigious country clubs during my tenure at Oak Hill CC, including Augusta National Golf Club, PGA National Resort, Calusa Pines Golf Club, Pinehurst Resort, and so forth, just to mention a few. These companies were contracted for their services by country clubs, therefore sending many caddie masters (employees of the country club) and some caddies to the unemployment line.

Perhaps the greatest difference between caddies employed as independent contractors and caddies working for the likes of Caddie Services Inc., Caddiemaster, and other such companies was that the independent contractor had the responsibility of paying his own taxes (of which 99 percent do not), while those working for certified organizations receive weekly or biweekly checks with all taxes being withheld. It is my belief that the same is true with professional tour caddies.

Tipping

Perhaps the greatest factor in a caddie's overall payment for his services is the tip. This gratuity is based on many different categories such as presentation, skills, etiquette, behavior, knowledge, and so forth. Obviously, the honor caddie will generate more in financial rewards due to their experience. Throughout my career as Caddie Master, a good tip would be about half the caddie's rate as stated on the chit or caddie report card. For example, if a caddie's rate was $50 per bag, a payment in the $140–$160 range for a double would be considered adequate. Anything less than $140 would be worth examination; more than $150 would be considered generous. In some cases, if a golfer played above and beyond his expectations, perhaps he would just happen to tip extremely well, regardless of the caddie's classification and performance.

Two Extremes

Let me share a couple of instances on both sides of tipping and the caddies' thinking. Back in 2004, when the rates were low (I mean pitifully low), I had a relatively new, first-year A caddie who complained because he only received $60 for a double bag, which was legitimate but within the guidelines. His rate at the time was $20 per bag, plus a suggested tip of $5–$10, as printed on the chit. So I said, "What was the problem?"

His response? "I made $80 my last time out." To me, that means a) the member was generous, or b) he must have had a better day then; there could be several factors involved. So I negotiated with him. I would guarantee him $75 every time he doubled, provided certain conditions were satisfied. If he was paid $60, I would pay the difference of $15 out of my own pocket. If he made $100, he would owe me $25. Mind you, most honor caddies caddying double at this time would average $100 per double, which was considered good. The lad made an attempt to calculate what decision would be more beneficial to him.

Like every other caddie to whom I had made similar offers, he rejected my "fair deal." Never once did I experience a caddie returning money to the member or guest because he felt he had been overpaid. Case in point—in 2012, I assigned two honor caddies (ranked in the vicinity of #12–15 in the overall evaluation) to four unaccompanied guests. Their rate at the time was $50 per bag, plus gratuity (suggested at $10–$20 per bag). They would be paid $200 a piece by golfer #1 and another $200 again by golfer #2. They insisted on bringing it to my attention. Now these were not kids; one was a school teacher and the other was a golf instructor. Then they decided to wait it out for the generosity of the other two golfers.

I told them, "You two guys never made $400 for a double in your life, and to my knowledge, only my top two or three have been paid so generously."

Enough was enough. I requested they call it a day and return tomorrow. They agreed without comment. I later discovered, as one could logically calculate, these unaccompanied guests were high rollers from the Big Apple.

Recommended Tipping

I once read an article from *Golf Digest* that presented a guideline on tipping by members and guests at a typical private country club. The positions of those who should be compensated for their services included the Golf Service Center manager and his staff (separately), valet drivers, locker room attendants, the caddie master, caddies, waiters and waitresses, bartenders, and others involved in the service industry.

Being a Caddie Master, I was dumbfounded at what the suggested tip was recommended by the well-known publication. It stated twenty dollars per foursome (or five dollars per golfer). Now Oak Hill Country Club, with its history and prestige, was known for its long lists of guest play activity, some days exceeding fifty groups of golfers, the majority being foursomes. (Remember, there are two courses at Oak Hill). Tuesdays, Thursdays, and Fridays were the heaviest guest lists, with tee times every fifteen minutes from 7:00 a.m. to 11:00 a.m. and 2:00 p.m. to 5:00 p.m. (and later, if needed). The other days also had guest lists but not as extreme.

The majority of tee times consisted of one member and three guests. If walking caddies were not requested, a forecaddie would be assigned to the typical foursome. Many guests who golfed at Oak Hill CC never employed a caddie from a certified caddie program, though a large number of guests may have had their sons or daughters carry their bag. In this case, it gave me a great opportunity to showcase my talented workers. The majority of the time, the member would contact yours truly and usually request two honor doubles, and many had their preferences. There were also several members who desired to give their guests their own personal caddie and thus made an appeal for four singles. This is beneficial due to the fact that you have two extra sets of eyes to look for golf balls that had gone astray.

Getting back to tipping, caddies (especially honor caddies) did quite well when it came to their gratuity. There were many factors involved in calculating the tip, the two most important being performance and personality. Caddies who developed friendships with their golfers also fared well in terms of payment and future requests and assignments in the future.

Unfortunately, the Caddie Master did not fare as well at Oak Hill. The twenty dollars per foursome (or five dollars per golfer) as recommended in the article in a national prestigious golf publication (and posted in the Golf Service Center) was pure fantasy. There are many reasons for this, as I will explain.

First of all, contrary to the most popular misconception in caddie master-related issues, the caddie master cannot and does not accept or initiate kickbacks. This behavior is not accepted at any private club (of which I am aware). Even though it is quite financially lucrative, it usually concludes with the caddie master's termination. Secondly, many members and guests have never really employed a caddie (or caddies) and therefore are not knowledgeable when it comes to payment and gratuity. A great percentage of golfers need a chit for a reference, or they approach other members, guests, or even employees of the club in regard to a caddie's salary and gratuity. Nowhere on the chit, in the Gold Book, or other media is there any mention of gratuity for the caddie master. Third of all, no one is aware of this practice although it is very common at the other Top 100 country clubs in the United States.

Let me give you an example. The general manager had me research other private clubs in the northeastern part of the country to compare salaries of caddie masters. Now these were small market private clubs with none being rated in *Golf Digest*'s Top 100. Obviously, what they were paying the Caddie Master at Oak Hill Country Club was right in line with the lesser-known clubs. Also, the general manager stated that tipping was not a major benefit at these other country clubs I had no idea where he obtained this information. My knowledge and research into this matter indicated quite the opposite: he was comparing apples to oranges.

One autumn, on my way to Florida to stay until the following golf season, I stopped by a country club that would be hosting the 2007 US Open to check out their caddie program. Back then, a member at this prestigious club had to employ a caddie; carts were only for those individuals physically unable to walk the golf course. I believe since then the policy has been somewhat altered.

So I inquired of the caddie master there about the number of caddies in his program. He stated two hundred seventy! When I further questioned him on how he trained all those caddies, he replied, "I don't. I just send them out there." Now I was aware that this country club had a well-established caddie program. Who wouldn't want to caddy at a club that has hosted more US Opens than any other golf or country club in the country? Not to mention that the wage for caddies was substantially higher than at Oak Hill. Another practice that I noticed at this club was when the member handed the caddie master the chit after the round was completed (all payment for the caddies at this club was done by this method), he would mention to bump the figure another $20, $30, $50, or whatever for the caddie master's gratuity! This rarely was the case at Oak Hill CC.

Kickbacks?

In my beginning days as the Caddie Master, when I assigned some caddies in the early spring from my more limited pool of caddies, some showed their appreciation by passing on monetary gifts to their supervisor. These tips were neither required nor a condition of their employment. A member's son, who happened to have been grandfathered into the present caddie program, stated that I was accepting kickbacks. It has always been, to my knowledge and understanding, that a kickback was a percentage of the earnings a caddie received that would be surrendered to the caddie master, with or without a caddie's consent. It was brought to Craig Harmon's attention, and he wanted to discuss the issue. After I explained my philosophy on the subject and after extensive questioning from the head pro, Mr. Harmon informed me that I would no longer be able to accept gratuities from Oak Hill caddies. Even though the Caddie Master was only making $12.50 per hour (yes, you read that right—$12.50 cash money an hour), I agreed that I would no longer be taking monetary tips from my workers. Case closed.

Benefits for Members' Children Working as Caddies

Another problem that arises when you have members' sons caddying is the rules of the caddie yard become compromised. Caddies must wait at least three hours to earn their points for the days if they do not get a loop. A caddie also earns points for caddying according to the grade on their report card. These points are added up at the conclusion of the period to reward those with good attendance and performance.

So the sons of members who caddied would wait perhaps for an hour or two and then (if they didn't think they would get a loop) grab their clubs from the storage area of the Golf Service Center. They would then proceed to the driving range or head over to the first hole, provided they possessed the proper bag tag. Different color tags dictated what privileges these members' sons had in regards to playing golf. White bag tags indicated the paying member, and these were associated with the most benefits and the least restrictions.

Obviously, this privilege did not sit well with the other caddies, who could only play on Mondays (no practice range) if there wasn't a corporate outing, some type of qualifier, a Western New York Professional Golf Association (WNYPGA) event, etc. Outside of Augusta National Golf Club (where caddies can only golf once a year, I believe), I am not aware of many clubs with these tight restrictions of their caddies playing golf. Not only that, caddies cannot ride carts, which, in a way, makes sense since their income and livelihood is based on carrying golf clubs around the golf course. Another benefit is that a member, but most likely a friend of his, would request a member's son to caddie for him. Some members who had sons in the program didn't always employ caddies, and one or two rarely used any caddies at all! I even had one of these grandfathered-in caddies who refused to caddie for his own father because his father's acquaintance paid better.

Locker Room Incident

What generated the above investigation on my behalf was a complaint I received from Jack, the locker room manager, that caddies had been seen roaming the locker room. Some members complained to Jack that personal items were missing from their lockers. Now Jack knew they were caddies because the ones observed in the locker room were wearing caddie bibs. So Jack concluded (wrongly) that caddies were stealing from the members. The only thing Jack was not aware of was if a nonmember caddie was seen in the clubhouse, he would forfeit his employment at Oak Hill CC as an independent contractor. Since money earned caddying paid better than most other jobs at this stage of their lives, the punishment far outweighed the benefits from stealing. If anything was missing, I told him to then question the individuals in the locker room. I never heard another word from Jack again relating to this matter.

Early Caddie Application

In the spring of 2014, I received an email from a student at a local private high school (where approximately one hundred members from Oak Hill CC were alumni), stating he possessed an interest in becoming a caddie during the upcoming season. Unfortunately, this lad submitted his application on March 12th, 2014, much earlier than the requested posted date of April 15th. I believe he thought because of his outside connections to a member, this gave him "privileged" status.

The Letter

My reaction at first was "Are you kidding me?" The problem was that the email sent from the Caddie Master went viral. When anyone sends someone else a personal letter or email, it's only common courtesy (well it was, as I was taught) that the communication was meant to be between those two individuals. But this doesn't appear to be true in today's world of information technology. And as I stated in my response to the job applicant, I was just being sarcastic.

This became a case of a third, fourth, or whatever kind of party interpreting it the wrong way. It appears that this email struck a nerve with some member whose nephew (from the knowledge I had gathered) was one of the applicant's best friends.

I purposely set a date on the caddie page of the Oak Hill CC website with the intention of not being bothered in Florida with my employment up north since it would not commence until mid-April. Also, I was employed at another country club in Tequesta, Florida, during the winter months. On top of that, the training sessions did not begin until mid-May. Where was their consideration?

And what about the source? The problem here was that when I became the Caddie Master in 2003, certain rules were not being followed, especially the one relating to the use of forecaddies (Oak Hill Country Club Gold Book, Section "Caddies," page 34). The policy is plain and simple. I took it upon myself (and as part of my responsibilities as Caddie Master) to enforce the code as published in the Oak Hill "bible."

Unfortunately, many members chose not to familiarize themselves with the Gold Book and were not content with the fact that a forecaddie would be assigned to their group since only one member in the foursome was present. Even when the practice had been in effect for some time, a few golfers (usually younger members) would request a tee time with two guests and then proceed to bring a third for the sole purpose of not having to employ a forecaddie, purely for financial reasons (too cheap). After all, it may cost the member a C-note or whatever, and that saving could be invested in adult beverages. "You're a member at Oak Hill and you can't afford $100 to help a student pay his tuition?" I would ask (rhetorically, of course).

There was one instance that specifically comes to mind when this unethical maneuver almost ruined my fair and honest character. I recall it was a Thursday afternoon in midsummer; a 2:15 p.m. tee time with Mr. X and his supposedly two guests. Well, you guessed it! He had invited another guest to complete his foursome without informing the pro shop or the Caddie Master.

As fate would have it, Ms. L. F. (who was a paying member and tipped better than most of her male counterparts; in fact, she was the only female golfer to compensate the Caddie Master) occupied the next tee time with her three guests. Lo and behold, I was contacted by the starter at the first hole of the East Course because Ms. L. F. had a grievance, and rightfully so.

"Why is it that I have to have a forecaddie while Mr. X does not?" she complained, livid.

Now it was customary for me to always assign a forecaddie to any member and three guests (or any unaccompanied guests, regardless of the number of golfers). Unfortunately, at that time, all my caddies were already employed and there were no other workers available in the caddie yard. It's not that the woman didn't want a forecaddie (she always requested a couple of honor caddies in particular), she just wanted a legitimate reason why the other foursome was allowed to proceed without one. After I explained to her that the other member had not informed the respective parties and I had no other caddies available, she was still not satisfied. She gave me an earful! Boy, was she ticked! But how was I to blame? Just another chapter in the life of a caddie master of which people are unaware.

I was Caddie Master for eleven seasons for Craig Harmon. I will always remember my final day of the 2011 season. It was my yearly custom to bid farewell to some of my fellow employees before I headed south to my residence in Florida. I stated to Mr. Harmon that, God willing, I would be seeing him next spring. Craig stunned me when he said, "Joe, it has been a pleasure having you as a member of my staff all these years." Mr. Harmon was not one known to hand out compliments to fellow employees at Oak Hill CC. I was flabbergasted. As I stated earlier, I will never forget that moment as long as I live.

It is true that I always expected to return year after year; I was never told otherwise, nor was it ever mentioned that my position as Caddie Master was ever in jeopardy. From the feedback of management, the head pro, members, and many guests, I was more than efficient in the performance of my profession. It was also mentioned to me by several members and guests who have played golf on many of the finest courses in the country and in the world that the caddie program at Oak Hill CC was second to none. And I almost never heard anything negative about the caddie program I conducted—or the Caddie Master himself.

Politics in Caddie Selection

In several circumstances at the beginning of a new golf season at the club, I would be approached by members and employees alike to consider certain individuals as new caddies in the program. Since a miniscule number of applicants would come under consideration, mainly due to the number of returning veteran caddies, it was impossible to select all the candidates who wished to become caddies at Oak Hill Country Club. Obviously, members who employed caddies frequently were given priority status.

Most of the new caddies that I selected were solely my decision, a decision based on their background, skills, etiquette, and my analysis of their performance during the training sessions and their final exam results.

Unfortunately, on some rare occasions, I would be coerced to include new individuals into the caddie program due solely to politics, usually favors for employees in the upper echelon at the club to friends or other acquaintances. This is not a practice with which I was comfortable, even though in most cases, it was favorable to the Caddie Master and the program when the person involved proved to be well-disciplined and respectful to authority and his peers.

Craig Harmon never persuaded or forced me to hire anyone in particular, but he kindly approached me to see if I would consider a couple of young gentlemen. These two individuals became excellent additions to the caddie program.

Now on the other hand, I was given no real choice but to allow the son of an extremely high-positioned employee into the program. He was a well-behaved high school boy, but I do not believe that, even though he attended all the training sessions, he actually absorbed any of the material and information that was presented in class or on the golf course. He flunked miserably on the easy caddie exam with the lowest score I had ever observed in my career as the Caddie Master.

This "choice" resulted in a very negative effect on the entire caddie program, as all the other caddies realized and commented on the issue. Unfortunately, my hands were tied.

After about a month of his service in the caddie program, I was able to locate his father in the parking lot of the club (some distance from the clubhouse) to address him regarding this unpleasant situation. We conversed for one half hour, discussing the fact that, his son, even though a fine lad, was a terrible caddie. However, he never offered what I believed to be the obvious solution, that being a recommendation from him to relieve his son of his duties, even though he realized that the caddie program at Oak Hill CC was suffering from his child's inclusion. Even though I do dislike seeing this happen to anyone, this high-ranking employee did not receive a contract for the following golf season and the issue resolved itself.

Oak Hill Country Club Caddie Program

Caddies at Oak Hill Country Club

Caddies at Oak Hill Country Club came from a very diversified group. No two were alike, not even close. For the most part, the caddie program consisted mainly of mature young men. They came in all shapes and sizes, but most were in fine physical shape, largely due to caddying and their training at their respective gyms or athletic training centers.

From all my experiences with caddies all over the country and caddie masters, it was easy to say that, as a group, (most) caddies were likely to imbibe alcoholic beverages, and the ones at Oak Hill CC were no exception. Due to early morning tee times, I lost several caddies due to missed assignments. Other caddies did not prefer to attend to work the mandatory three days per week, and they were terminated. Still others who had been admitted into the caddie program really didn't have the desire to work at all or further their caddie skills necessary to reach honor status; they just wanted to get paid and would be the first to bitch about not being compensated as they believed they were entitled. This caliber of caddies did not last because of the standards I had set and their lack of initiative and responsibility.

Most caddies realized that the wages for caddying and the potential for good gratuities were not easily matched at other sources of summer employment; in addition, if your work and character were above satisfactory, it would be a good measure of job security.

To provide you with an insight to some of the individual caddies I had in the caddie program, I will share more about certain characters.

Caddie Backgrounds

For the most part, my caddies ranged in age from sixteen to sixty. Most of the caddies had a comfortable living, being that the majority of them lived in the suburbs. In my twelve years as Caddie Master, there were perhaps only about a dozen who caddied in the program who did not live in the suburbs; most of them were of African American descent. The African American caddies, for the most part, were career-seasoned veterans. Although they were very knowledgeable about the game, they never golfed on Monday (with one exception). Mondays were designated as employee and caddie golf days, but they often preferred to work in the afternoon if there was some activity. On many Mondays, there would be corporate outings, where no employees or caddies would be allowed to play golf unless it was early in the morning or after the event.

The East Course was always the stage for the golfing part of the outing, with one exception, and that being the Golisano Children's Hospital fundraiser. If there was a Monday where an outing was not scheduled, the East Course was closed until two o'clock for maintenance, usually followed by a guest list as long as time would allow.

In the "old days" (when I caddied there in my younger years), the clubhouse was closed on Mondays, as was the norm for most private clubs in the country. I am not aware of the year when this changed, but basically, the East Course was closed until 2:00 p.m., and the West was just about always open, with some exceptions (WNYP-GA events, tournament qualifiers, RDGA (Rochester District Golf Association) events, McQuaid Golf (a local high school), and so forth). The only reasons for closing the courses (especially the East) were due to nature (flooding, snow, lighting), aerification of the courses, or national championships.

Getting back to the caddies, while I was Caddie Master, there were many diverse backgrounds and geographic locations represented in the caddie program at Oak Hill CC. On my roster were caddies from Georgia, Illinois, Ohio, Florida, Colorado, Pennsylvania, Alabama, Hawaii, and several other states. I also had requests from Scotland, Ireland, and England from people interested in caddying at Oak Hill.

Late in the season (especially in Northeast), say mid-August to early October, caddies became scarce because so many returned to academia. It was during this time that caddie masters struggled to meet the demand. I was fortunate enough to acquire anywhere from three to six caddies from the Secession Golf Club in Beaufort, Georgia. The reason for this was due to weather conditions, mainly the heat of the summer, in the South that resulted in many country clubs closing their respective golf courses. Consequently, these mostly lifetime caddies were searching for employment somewhere.

So I contacted Mr. G. C., the caddie master at Secession Golf Club, to get background checks, as was my procedure with any caddies transferring from other country clubs. The purpose was to find good caddies who would not be detrimental to the Oak Hill CC caddie program. Caddie masters have a mutual respect for each other and will inform them if caddies they are considering for a position in their program are worthy or not.

Schoolteachers

As previously mentioned, caddies at Oak Hill ranged in age from sixteen to sixty, and their profiles were quite diverse. In any given year, my roster would contain anywhere from eight to twelve schoolteachers, including golf coaches, and even a professor with a doctorate in sports management.

Many realized caddying was a great summer job. Being in that profession meant that a notable number of these instructors could make over a thousand dollars a week as a caddie at Oak Hill CC and enjoy golfing there on Mondays when the courses were available. Also, the money obtained from caddying, plus any and all gratuities, was tax-free unless the caddies claimed this income on their 1040 forms, which I doubt ever occurred. The most positive benefit of having schoolteachers as caddies was their maturity and dependability.

Students

Roughly two-thirds of the caddie program consisted of high school and college students. They attended academic institutions all over the country, including Ivy League and other prestigious colleges such as the University of Rochester, Notre Dame, Ohio State, Dayton, Penn State, Michigan State, Auburn, Florida State, and a multitude of other institutions of higher learning. It was a great privilege to observe these "kids" throughout their caddie years eventually becoming brain surgeons, architects, teachers, brokers, accountants, Wall Street executives, entrepreneurs, and so forth.

B

B was my number one caddie for all the years I was at the helm as the Caddie Master at Oak Hill Country Club. He rarely had to bide his time in the caddie yard for a loop because he was constantly requested by members and guests alike. A good family man, he was originally from Columbus, Ohio, and had worked as a professional caddie for many years on the Ladies Professional Golf Association (LPGA) Tour.

B possessed all the skills necessary for being a professional caddie. I have heard many stories relating to his workmanship on the LPGA Tour from many women professionals. There are a couple I remember from our discussions and conversations.

The first I recall was Moira Dunn; B had toted her bag for a lengthy time. After 244 tournaments on the LPGA Tour, she was finally victorious in 2004. Unfortunately, she would never visit the winner's circle again. The other LPGA Tour professional worth mentioning was the ever-controversial Christina Kim. I believe B caddied for her at some points in the peak of her career and just before she took a hiatus from the Tour for personal reasons.

In the professional golf business, players and caddies are always negotiating contracts. In B's case, I am aware that finances sometimes become an issue, as well as a stumbling block.

There were other instances in B's caddying career at Oak Hill CC that are impossible for a Caddie Master to forget.

The first situation involved his caddying for Mr. T., a lawyer very well-known at this country club. Now it has been said (according to one member I will not identify) that Oak Hill CC had a reputation as being a hard-drinking, heavy gambling club in many golf circles. I don't know about the gambling aspect, but from my observations, the high consumption of adult beverages has a good chance of being an affirmative assumption.

So anyway, B and Mr. T. were on the ninth hole of the East Course one summer day, and Mr. T. and B agreed on the yardage to the flagstick. Mr. T. questioned B on which club he should hit, a 5 wood versus a 3 iron. This par four (like so many Donald Ross-designed courses) is a signature crowned narrow green that slopes off steeply on the left side of the green and possesses a couple of well-placed sand traps on the right.

B persuaded Mr. T. into selecting the 5 wood. He nailed the shot "right on the screws" and said to his caddie, "You better be [expletive] right. I have fifteen thousand at stake on this hole!" I believe that Mr. T. won his bet, even though I never heard either positively or negatively on the result. B never mentioned the outcome or how much he was compensated.

Another episode in B's illustrious career occurred in 2008 in the annual prestigious amateur championship, known as the John R. Williams Tournament, a two-man best ball event held in mid-September. My best caddie was requested by two Canadian golfers, and B caddied for these eventual winners.

Before the tournament even began, Mr. W., one of the contestants, handed some money to his caddie and said, "Let's get started, let's get to work." Everything went well for the Canadians throughout the tournament. In the final round, they proceeded to hole-out on eighteen and anxiously waited for the second-place contestants, one stroke behind them in the fight for the championship. The challengers had about a twenty-five-foot birdie putt they needed to drop to force a playoff. Fortunately for B and his golfers, the putt failed to be converted, and the team of Mr. W. and Mr. H. was victorious.

Sometime after the tournament had ended and the champions had been presented with their trophy, B approached Mr. W. and offered his caddie services and the opportunity to work for them in the 2009 John R. Williams Tournament as defending champions. Mr. W. gladly accepted his caddie's offer but explained that he would not be competing in the following year. He had stage IV cancer and had been given only six more months to live. He died the following February at the age of fifty-one.

B and Pappy

There were two caddies in the Oak Hill CC at that time who were always requested, many times as a pair. They were seasoned veterans in their forties. B had spent his earlier years as a professional caddie on the LPGA Tour and another individual I will refer to as Pappy. The former was just a tad more skillful (being a professional), whereas the latter possessed a more outgoing personality.

Pappy

In the spring of 2004, Mr. C. R., the liaison between the member-ship and the caddie program contacted the Caddie Master via cell phone to request that I give his kid, who desired to become an Oak Hill caddie, a look. I agreed to meet with this young gentleman the following day in the caddie yard for an interview.

Well as fate would have it, he arrived as scheduled the next day, looking for the Caddie Master. He introduced himself and stated that Mr. C. R. told him to see me personally. Now this "kid" was about six-foot three, tilting the scales at about 280 pounds. He in-formed me that he was a retired NJ state trooper and even played in the National Football League during the 1987 players-strike season as a replacement (he was what many referred to as a "scab"). He was built like a brick shithouse (excuse the expression) with arms as big as his thighs. This was one hell of a big kid.

Although he had never caddied before, Pappy knew the game of golf and, just like every other caddie who played the game, was very knowledgeable and familiar with its rules, regulations, and etiquette. It only took a minimal amount of time for him to develop into one of the top caddies at Oak Hill CC.

Pappy also possessed a unique personality, second to no other caddie at the club; he was very outgoing, personable, knowledgeable, and witty, but most of all, he was so friendly and giving. He was a good family man and a very caring and generous person; he would do anything for anyone. Let me give you an example.

There was an honor caddie at Oak Hill who was a tremendous forecaddie and ran like a gazelle, the best forecaddie in the entire program and always in great demand for his forecaddying skills. For some reason, the caddies nicknamed him "Scoobie."

Now it is my belief that Scoobie, who was a devout and practicing Christian, gave all his money to those less fortunate than himself. He was always borderline when it came to the dress code (white shirt, khaki shorts or slacks, decent sneakers or golf shoes—an overall nice appearance). I had a difficult time believing he possessed an iron and an ironing board, much less a comb.

One day, he just went too far according to my standards. He appeared for his assignment, and his sneakers appeared to have been his dog's intended lunch, gaping holes in each one. I mentioned to him that his wardrobe was unacceptable, and I needed to see some improvement.

Pappy happened to be there while I was addressing Scoobie. He stated that he would bring in a couple pairs of new sneakers the following day, and he upheld his promise (though that was no real shock to me).

In the meantime, Scoobie appeared for his loop with a different pair of sneakers, which he had possessed for quite some time. They were in no better condition than the other pair I had previously condemned. Later, he graciously accepted the two pairs of new sneakers that Pappy provided and was ever so thankful.

The day after he received the new sneakers, Scoobie arrived for his scheduled assignment. Now, believe it or not, he is not wearing either of the pairs of shoes that Pappy had given him but another old pair of sneakers in need of much repair. Anyway, as I recall, he was travaling cross-country the following day to do some serious hiking, so I just let the situation slide. Like I had previously mentioned, he was a great caddie, it was late in the year, and I was limited in personnel to fill his shoes, so what was I supposed to do?

I never did find out what became of those two new pair of sneakers, but it is my belief that he probably donated them to someone less fortunate who was unable to afford shoes themselves, but it had been my hope, for his own benefit and appearance, that he would decide to claim ownership.

With Pappy's personality and charisma, it was not difficult for him to be liked by everyone, male and female alike. One occasion in particular comes to mind.

There was a member from Oak Hill CC who also happened to possess property and belong to a private country club in Naples, Florida. She had invited three of her girlfriends from down South to accompany her in playing golf on the Championship Course. Now Mrs. D. R. was a good golfer in her own right, many times walking and toting her Sunday bag herself on her five-foot frame. And that was being generous!

The timing of this foursome occurred early in my career as the Caddie Master. As I had previously mentioned earlier in the book, the forecaddie provision from the Oak Hill Country Club Gold Book states that "any member with three guests must employ a forecaddie."

Now the member proceeded to inform me she really didn't need nor want a forecaddie. I politely replied that I was just trying to do my job and enforcing the statutes as written by the board of directors (or whoever held responsibility). Many members—mostly men—questioned the Caddie Master with the same reasoning. The problem here, as with most country clubs, was that no one reads or familiarizes themselves with the book of rules and policies.

To continue on with the foursome of women, I mentioned to Mrs. D. R. that the forecaddie fee (at that time) was fifty dollars, plus tip. Needless to say, at the conclusion of the round, the group was extremely elated with Pappy's performance. Not only did they pay him quite handsomely, but they also included him as the centerpiece for their group photograph on the signature thirteenth hole of the East Course!

As mentioned previously, Pappy was always in great demand, especially at tournament time, and the Men's Invitational was the main event. In the first couple of years, Pappy caddied for different members and their guests. One year, there was a bidding war for his services. Mr. S. finally offered to pay Pappy one thousand dollars, and he was the winner. Outside of the top honor caddies at Oak Hill, the average for the other caddies in the Men's Invitational was perhaps in the $375–$425 range (before the playoff, known as the Shootout). This was easy money. The format was seven nine-hole matches against the other teams in your flight. Most of the caddies forecaddied for their team, several driving the golf cart as the players walked. Some other golfers had their caddies carry bags. However, you do the math, the caddies did quite well for sixty-three holes.

Then there was the Dr. John R. Williams Tournament (as mentioned earlier) hosted annually by Oak Hill CC. The good doctor was an arborist who was responsible for the planting of the hundreds of oak trees that adorn the two beautiful golf courses at Oak Hill Country Club.

It was my belief that this tournament was by invitation only. Most contestants had extensive golf résumés and credentials, and many were scratch golfers.

One of the regular entrants in this prestigious tournament took a liking for Pappy the first time they were introduced to each other. Mr. G. was from Macon, Georgia, and as I recall, he had a very lucrative position in the financial world.

Now Pappy had become Mr. G.'s right-hand man; he did just about everything. His responsibilities included not only caddying for Mr. G. and his golfing partner, but also caring for the clubs and baggage, familiarizing himself with their itinerary, such as what time to pick them up at the airport, where to go for cocktails and dinner, tee times, practice schedules, and so forth. Pappy excelled in everything he did; he was punctual, courteous, comical—just a great guy to be associated with.

Pappy was compensated quite generously by Mr. G., as was likely with everyone for whom he caddied. He was also well respected by the employees at the club, such as the general manager, Craig Harmon, his fellow caddies, the Caddie Master, and the members and guests. I was well aware that there were some other caddies who made him uncomfortable, but he would never belittle anyone publicly.

There was a certain honor caddie, N. G., who worked well as a team with Pappy. On many occasions, they caddied together, usually as doubles. They had a mutual respect for each other and were familiar with each other's work ethic. They were such a great team and caddying partners together. They even had their picture posted on the front page of the local newspaper after caddying for some members and their guests just before the PGA Championship at Oak Hill CC in 2013. I had no greater respect for any caddie other than Pappy.

Mack

On one occasion in October of 2013, I received a request for two honor double caddies for four unaccompanied guests at 7:00 a.m. on the East Course. At this time, the greens fees for said golfers was four hundred dollars per person per round. A request of this nature usually resulted in a generous gratuity for the Caddie Master. As I mentioned earlier, there were no backups or caddies milling around the caddie yard in late summer waiting for work. The caddies who were available were all assigned, and on many occasions, they were assigned for two rounds on any given day.

Well, I took a gamble and assigned two honor caddies who were both moderate to heavy drinkers. But one was always punctual, and the other hadn't missed an assignment in over a year. At 6:30 a.m. the following morning, I asked Pappy if he had talked to Mack about their loop. They had caddied together on numerous occasions. Pappy assured me Mack would be there. 7:00 a.m. arrived, and there was only one caddie present.

Most golfers capable of walking will just about always do so on a venue such as Oak Hill East; as I had been informed by many, especially guests, they did so to "enhance the full experience, to follow the path on the Championship Course as so many touring pros have done in the past." So the unaccompanied guests made the decision that they would reluctantly ride in golf carts and use the one assigned honor caddie as a forecaddie, due to the unforeseen circumstances. Obviously, the caddie in attendance was ticked because being employed in this role, on most occasions, results in a lower payday than if he had worked as a double. To sum up, I had failed to satisfy the guests' request, thus resulting in negating a handsome gratuity.

I attempted to communicate with Mack via cell phone but was unsuccessful at least on a dozen occasions. He finally contacted me at 9:30 a.m. to say that he had overslept. Are you kidding me? The other caddie and I had suffered financial losses, and did Mack really believe I was not aware of his abuse of alcohol and other mind-altering drugs? I had been aware of his drinking problem for some time, but lately it had been brought to my attention that he was experimenting with pills. At that time, I had assumed it was opiates, which had become so prevalent at that time. It was no mistake; I was well aware of this caddie's situation and his weaknesses. At this time of the golfing season, that was the gamble I had to take. Unfortunately, for the foursome of unaccompanied guests, the forecaddie, and the Caddie Master, all had a negative experience because of one's inability to perform and his total disregard for responsibility. Mack had presented me with no other choice than to terminate him from the caddie program. Let's face it—in reality, caddies always make the final decision. Many end their careers thanks to their sophomoric decisions.

Lyle

I'll share another circumstance of a caddie forfeiting his employment because of his bad habit. In this case, it was just a couple of
beers, so he said. Lyle was forecaddying for a group on Men's Special
Guest Day. That was an occasion once a month where a member
could invite three, seven, or eleven guests. The costs were basically
one, two, or three thousand dollars, depending on the number of
foursomes, obviously. During these events, kegs of beer were positioned around the golf course. Mr. Z. informed me at the end of his
round that Lyle had been observed imbibing on a different hole; he
had been forecaddying for a different foursome.

Lyle finished forecaddying about half an hour later. When I approached him to discuss his beer-drinking on the course, he did not
deny it, much to my surprise.

So I said to him, "You are aware that you cannot consume alcoholic beverages while you are caddying; every caddie knows that!"

To which he replied, "I was thirsty."

Needless to say, next to the keg were coolers containing assorted
sodas, juices, and water, plus an assortment of snacks. In the end,
I had him surrender his caddie bib and exclaimed that he was no
longer a part of the Oak Hill CC caddie program.

Walter

Abuse of drugs and alcohol were not the only methods for ending one's career as a caddie on my roster. Let me give another prime example. Walter introduced himself to the Caddie Master in the caddie yard sometime in June 2009. He had attended a prestigious local high school and claimed to be a good friend of one of my honor caddies, who attended the same institution and who also happened to be a scratch golfer and a member of a well-known golfing family in the Greater Rochester area. I concluded that Walter was in his late twenties, early thirties, just looking for work. After we had had a conversation for about half an hour, he informed me that he caddied at the Seminole Golf Club in Juno Beach, Florida. Since I lived in Stuart, Florida, I was quite familiar with the area. Then he continued to mention that he had caddied over two hundred rounds at the renowned country club, which had always been rated the number one golf course in the state of Florida and consistently mentioned in the top echelon of *Golf Digest*'s Top 100 golf courses in the United States.

If he was good enough to caddy at Seminole GC, I figured he had to be an excellent candidate to caddy at Oak Hill CC. Since the time was early June and the majority of my caddies were either attending or teaching school, I was limited on available bodies. As I mentioned earlier, when I obtained caddies at that club from other country clubs, I would contact the acting caddie master. I would usually perform a background check, but this time, I neglected to do so. But his résumé, coupled with me being short on available caddies this time of year, convinced me to assign him to forecaddie for a member and his three guests.

After a short stint at the range, the group proceeded to the first tee of the East Course. I noticed Walter sprinting ahead of them, so I figured everything was just fine. As I did with all new caddies who came into the program, I had given him an approximately a one-hour tour of the layout, emphasizing landing areas, location of sprinkler heads (which indicate distances to the green), trouble spots, and so forth. I'd had Walter shadow me earlier in the day, so his memory should have been somewhat fresh.

After about an hour and a half into his round, I decided to grab a Club Car, and, armed with my field glasses, I went to observe how well the transferred caddie was performing. As I arrived at the eighth hole, Walter was nowhere to be found. I crossed from the roadside of the hole (the right side from the tee) to the other side, a heavily wooded area between the seventh and eighth holes, only to find the "seasoned" caddie walking through the forest!

"Wouldn't you get a better view from the left side of the rough?" I asked.

"Oh, probably," he stated as he headed toward the eighth fairway. I didn't need to see any more at this point and returned to the caddie yard for other business.

Unfortunately, I was not able to further observe Walter on this day. I approached the member and his guests as they made their way back to the Golf Service Center and the caddie yard to finalize their round (recording scores, taking care of their belongings, finishing their beers, settling their debts, like most golfers did at the end of their rounds).

"And how was your forecaddie?" I addressed the member.

"Very green" was his reply. I explained to Mr. J. S. that the caddie was new at Oak Hill and that it was his first round forecaddying on the Championship Course. "Well, he's definitely going to need a few more rounds to become efficient, especially to fit in your program," he exclaimed.

"Thank you, sir. I will work on it," I told him. Not music to my ears, as I was used to receiving, but I decided to give Walter another chance.

The following day, I received a request from Mr. I. for four single caddies for a group of golfers, one member and his three guests. I explained to the member that a couple of the caddies may lack some experience. He agreed to allow those in question to caddy, to help out the caddie program. (A fair percentage of the members who used caddies regularly would do this early in the season.)

I proceeded to assign to this group an honor caddie, an A caddie, a B caddie, and Walter. When the eighteen holes had been completed, I had the member and the honor caddie rate the others on their performance. Together, we discussed what had transpired on the golf course. The conclusion was not shocking, Walter was okay, but he ranked last of the four caddies. Following that conference, I returned to the caddie area and relaxed my weary body to have a chat with Walter. Now, Walter was no kid, and, according to him, he had been around golf his entire life to one degree or another. So I stated to Walter that I had concluded all his caddying expertise seemed very limited. He then reiterated that he had caddied over two hundred rounds at the Seminole Golf Club in Juno Beach, Florida. It was then that I decided to interrogate him.

"What is the name of the caddie master at Seminole?"

"How would I know?" was his reply.

I further quizzed him. "How can you sit there and make me believe that you caddied over two hundred rounds at this great country club and cannot even name the person in charge of the caddie program?" He shrugged his shoulders. I shot back, "How about the name of the head golf professional?"

"I never met him" was his reply.

To say the least, just about anyone familiar with the golf scene knew that Bob Ford arguably had one of the best jobs in the country club life (and perhaps the country)—that is, head golf professional at Oakmont CC in the summer and the same position at Seminole Golf Club in the winter. What a living! Needless to say, this wannabe Oak Hill caddie had experienced his last moments on that sacred turf.

Randy

Randy, a young college student, was an excellent golfer and a member of the Nazareth College golf team. He achieved honor caddie, and he was just a respectful and fine individual, a very well disciplined and a fun-loving character.

One evening after a double loop at Oak Hill CC, Randy returned to his residence to shower and freshen up for a night on the town with other friends and caddies. They decided to entertain themselves in the high-end district known to attract millennials, the younger generation of college students, and all types of diverse people from that cultural district.

After several hours of socializing, Randy decided it would be in his best interests to segregate himself from the downtown locale to be ready for his caddie assignment the following morning. Unfortunately, when Randy went to unlock his automobile, he was confronted by an assailant who pressured Randy into surrendering his wallet at gunpoint.

At 6:45 a.m. the next day, Randy informed me of the circumstances from the previous evening. The caddie explained exactly what developed from the beginning to the end of his ordeal, including the disappearance of his personal property. Part of his belongings was a chit from the day before that had been presented to him by his player at the conclusion of the round.

"Well," I said to Randy, "obviously that "chit" is of no value to that individual who robbed you." I was familiar with the member for whom he had doubled on that occasion and how the member paid his honor caddie. If there was any happy ending to this incident, it was that Randy had $150 in his wallet that his mugger would not receive.

Super S. S.

Super S. S. had been a caddie before I came onto the scene as Caddie Master. He was a local boy with a deep Christian background. I believe his father was a doctor (of what I do not remember), and S. S. was a good kid, respectful toward his elders and his fellow caddies. Super S. S. did missionary work for his church and even traveled to Africa to spread the Word.

Super S. S. had been an honor caddie for several years before I met him. He knew his profession well and was extremely educated in it. Unfortunately, he possessed a desire to expand his bankroll; he seemed to have the impression he could not make enough. I didn't know what he did with his earnings (nor did I care; it was none of my business), but I doubt he contributed it all to charity. Perhaps he needed the money for college, who knows? Why would anyone be so obsessed with money if he was going to give it all away?

Anyway, one day, Super S. S. was out on a double loop for a member and his guest. Now, as Caddie Master, I had a policy that no one would caddy twice in any given day if there were other caddies available in the caddie yard who had not yet been assigned or able to get a job.

Super S. S. finished his loop and stated that Mr. L. wanted Super S. S. to caddy for him and his guest again on the West Course in the afternoon after lunch. I mentioned my policy of sharing the wealth to Mr. L. He stated that I was the Caddie Master and if that's the way it was, so be it. There was no further discussion on the matter.

Now Super S. S. was totally bent out of shape when I informed him that the decision had been made that "Polish Kid" would be doubling in about one hour's time for Mr. L. and his guest. Enraged as he was, Super S. S. yelled at me and said that he would discuss the matter with an assistant manager in the Golf Service Center. I had to explain to the irate caddie that the assistant manager had absolutely nothing to do with the caddie program, and that I alone was responsible for all caddie assignments and activities, training, hiring, firing, promotions, pay—you name it. Later, I discovered from an acquaintance familiar with this individual that he had informed him he ran the Golf Service Center and the caddie program at Oak Hill. As I stated, he had absolutely nothing to do with the caddie program at Oak Hill except for stealing the credit and recognition that I had created. For some reason, this character to whom I am referring also kept the tips given by members for the Golf Service Center's Annual Party in a "special fund." I never knew whatever became of this fund, since most of the food and drinks were donated by the kind membership. Dishonest as he was from the word "go," he was eventually terminated due to conduct unbecoming of an Oak Hill employee (nothing involving the annual party).

A few weeks later when Super S. S. came to his senses and I mentioned that to him to think about the role-reversal with the Polish Kid, he apologized. Honestly, I never did expect a caddie with his background to put me in a situation like that.

The Trouble

So there I was, sitting at home one summer evening in upstate New York, just off Canandaigua Lake, when I received a call on my cell phone. Since it was an employer-issued device, I figured I better answer it. On the other end of the line was a prominent member of Oak Hill CC who just happened to be an ex-president of this private establishment. He questioned me and finally asked me if I had a caddie who I had named Trouble. I answered that I only had one at the time, so I knew exactly to whom he was referring. (Trouble had the same first name as another caddie.)

Mr. R. had been relaxing in his library that evening reading a book when he heard a disturbance in his garage. He proceeded to the garage since he possessed several classic and antique automobiles that were stored there. When he opened the door to his garage and saw a young gentleman in there, he inquired what business he had in his garage.

To which the lad responded, "I know you, Mr. R. I caddied for you the other day. My name is Trouble."

Mr. R. insisted the caddie give him an explanation of what he was doing in his garage. It was my understanding (from my conversation with Mr. R.) that there was a heated argument and the caddie finally left. Mr. R. claimed the caddie was obnoxious, arrogant, belligerent, and appeared to be on something. I knew exactly to whom he was referring. Per his request, I gave him the caddie's last name. Mr. R. attempted to find his name in the phone book and discovered the college student lived a few blocks away. Then he contacted the caddie's father.

Upon returning to his garage sometime later, he noticed that his fire-engine-red Ferrari had been keyed! Are you kidding me? That dumbass kid keyed the guy's Ferrari! I couldn't believe what I was hearing!

Well, eventually the Monroe County Sheriff's Department was informed of the vandalism. Exactly what happened after that, I am not quite sure. I do know that on the following day, Trouble appeared in the caddie yard. He proceeded to move into the corner of the area, putting his back toward me. He was on his cell phone contacting someone. When he had entered the area, he had tossed his caddie bib on one of the tables, and I retrieved it. When his cell phone conversation came to a conclusion, I approached him to inform him that his caddie position at Oak Hill CC was being terminated.

"I don't understand. What happened last night has nothing to do with my job caddying!" he responded.

So quizzically, I asked him what would provoke him to exhibit such conduct, to which he answered that Mr. R.'s son owed him quite a substantial amount of money (about $2,600). "I just went over there with the intention of collecting what was owed to me," he explained.

Now I knew these young gentlemen both lived in a very affluent neighborhood; I knew they were wealthy. How did one teenager get himself into these financial situations? I concluded logically that I knew exactly what had occurred, and in a couple of weeks following, I learned I'd hit the nail right on the head.

Trouble and Casey

When I was appointed as the Caddie Master of Oak Hill Country Club, it was brought to my attention by the general manager and the member who was the liaison of the membership to the Caddie Master that I was obligated to retain those caddies who were members' offspring. According to the Oak Hill CC Gold Book, these caddies should not have been working at this country club in the first place. But since these individuals were already part of the caddie program, they would be grandfathered into my roster.

Now in this group of grandfathered-in caddies was a certain college student named Casey. He came from a well-established family and was respectful to the Caddie Master and all others in authority. Basically, he was a good kid, I was astonished to see him exhibiting a black eye when he appeared in the caddie yard for an assigned loop!

So naturally (and out of curiosity), I questioned the lad on the change of his facial appearance. He responded that he and his accomplice, Trouble, had been attacked by eight individuals at 2:30 a.m. in the morning on a street named Ambassador Drive, which just happens to be about the most prestigious and wealthiest neighborhood in Monroe County and only a few blocks from Oak Hill Country Club. Then he further explained that it cost him and Trouble eight hundred dollars—one hundred dollars per assailant—for the beating to be terminated. It sounded like a territorial war to me. Go figure.

A. R.

It was the spring of 2006 when I received a phone call from a life-time caddie in Georgia who was interested in extending his career at Oak Hill CC. This Southern gentleman had been caddying at the most prestigious country club in America, according to just about anyone who is familiar with the world of golf. Like many nomadic career caddies, his van was his home. He would travel from one destination to another, depending on location and the time of the year and what opportunities were available.

Eventually, I learned more of the life of A. R. It was revealed to me that he had originally found employment as a construction worker in Georgia but then decided that wasn't what he desired in life. I knew he had caddied at the world-renowned golf course, and he later informed me that he had issues with the caddie master at that location.

A. R. loved his music, and in his traveling home, one would find an assortment of stringed instruments, including a guitar, a banjo, and a mandolin. He even mentioned to me that he had jammed on several occasions with the legendary Forrest Richard Betts, better known as Dickey, a founding member and guitarist of the famous Allman Brothers Band. But there was one incident involving A. R. I simply will never forget.

I was contacted by A. R. in the winter of 2008. He stated that he was researching the possibility of caddying at some private country club in Florida, if and when the opportunity became available. Now, at that time, I held a position at the Tesoro Country Club in Palm City, Florida. It just so happened that the Tesoro Country Club was preparing to host their Men's Invitational. It was a scheduled three-day event, and the caddie master was searching for experienced forecaddies to fill his roster. The pay would be $240 per round, plus gratuities. Back in 2008, this would have been categorized as lucrative. So I presented the situation to A. R. and asked him if he was interested in working the tournament and if he would be available.

"Hell yeah" was his enthusiastic reply. And his next question was "Do you know of a place around the vicinity where I could get accommodations?" I informed him that I would look around and get back to him.

I began to think of how I could assist A.R. I finally presented it to my wife, who had very little knowledge of A. R. and/or his background. I mentioned his plight in life to her, and even though she was a bit leery, she hesitantly agreed that we would offer him a room at our home in Stuart. He was, to say the least, elated at our offer and generosity and immediately made plans to drive from Georgia to Florida. I had a liking for A. R., and he was a polite and well-mannered individual.

A. R. arrived the following afternoon prior to the actual opening round of the tournament. I invited the caddie into my modest residence and introduced him to my wife. I then proceeded to show him his own personal bedroom and bathroom before I headed to the kitchen to make preparations for a steak dinner. I offered him a predinner cocktail before the meal, but he declined, stating that he did not partake of alcoholic beverages.

As we assembled for dinner, we were conversing about life in general. A. R. shared his life story with my wife and I. He was not the brightest person I had ever met, and it didn't appear to me that he had attended any institution of higher learning. He never spoke of his childhood, and his married life was not ideal either. He was separated from his wife (she also possessed her own variety of personal problems), but they were the parents of four children and still maintained a somewhat friendly relationship between themselves and among their offspring. Then came the shocker.

My wife questioned our guest, "With a wife who has a limited income and four children, what do you do about health care?"

Now, at this particular time, my wife and I had both been in the workforce for over forty years (even with her taking four years off to raise our son and daughter), paid our mortgages, insurances, New York state taxes, and our health care, with other payments too numerous to mention.

A. R. chuckled as he responded, "We let people like you take care of that."

That reply was not what we were expecting, nor was it agreeable to either one of us. Even though my better half appeared to be calm, she was livid inside. We have always lived by the Golden Rule, but are you kidding me?

After three nights and three days, A. R. departed for another opportunity somewhere in the South. But before he left, he extended his gratitude to my wife and me for making his stay so comfortable. He even offered some money, but I refused, saying, "I believe you need the money more than us. Take care."

As time passed and my career at Oak Hill was in its last days, this same A. R. stopped me in person at the club and posed a question: "Hey, Joe, as you know, I am getting older. [He was probably in his late fifties.] I never put a dime into Social Security (or a 401(k), as far as I am aware). What am I going to do?"

Since I never had to deal with that situation personally, I just replied, "I honestly do not know." I had to bite my tongue and not say, "Let the government take care of you!"

Tyrone

Tyrone was an honor caddie throughout my career as Caddie Master. I wasn't sure of his combined number of years at Oak Hill CC before I started my career in 2002, but when I departed from those hallowed grounds, I approximated Tyrone was closing in on fifty years old. Outside of caddying, he spent his career as a physical education teacher at a local suburban high school.

As a high school employee not far from the country club, Tyrone acquainted himself with many of the parents of students he taught and came in contact with; it was only natural.

From my recollection of one story involving Tyrone, there was a member at Oak Hill CC who we referred to as Mr. T. C. For some reason, Tyrone became a good friend of Mr. T. C.'s, and occasionally they enjoyed a cocktail together.

Now, Mr. T.C happened to be a four-time All American wrestler from a large and prestigious university in upstate New York. I don't believe he weighed more than one hundred thirty pounds during his athletic career. Tyrone was a fine physical specimen himself; after all, he was a PE instructor. I would calculate about five foot ten inches and perhaps one hundred eighty pounds solid. On the other hand, the member was five foot five or six inches tall and probably somewhere around 145 pounds in weight. It was my belief they were similar in age.

It so happened they were at a social function, probably some sort of picnic, when, from what I had heard, the caddie was approached by the member, who stated that he would give Tyrone one hundred dollars if he could take him down as a reward for accomplishing the challenge. Realizing even though physically it would appear that Tyrone was the Goliath in this situation, he wisely retreated.

Now Mr. T. C. was persistent in coaxing Tyrone to take him down; he didn't have to pin him, just get him off his feet and on the ground. Two hundred dollars were offered and then four hundred dollars. Still Tyrone refused to budge.

Finally in frustration, Mr. T. C. said to the caddie, "Eight hundred dollars, and that will be my final offer." Remember, this was not a bet, and Tyrone decided why not? He had nothing to lose. What could Mr. T.C. possibly do to him? It was my understanding that alcohol could have been a contributing factor. The final end result did not come as a shock to me.

The next day, Tyrone appeared in the caddie area to cash an old chit. He had his right arm hanging in a sling due to a broken collarbone. When I inquired about what had happened, the story unfolded.

Thorn

As I had mentioned previously, like clockwork every new golf season, I would be approached by members to consider certain individuals as caddies at Oak Hill CC. This was the case with Mr. P. and his son, both members who used the caddie program quite extensively. They asked me if I would accept Thorn into the caddie program.

Now Thorn, who I eventually selected, was a very well-mannered high school student with a solid background in golf. He eventually became a decent A caddie, but due to his lack of attendance, he was unable to achieve the honor status; he was lacking in rounds of looping for possible advancement.

Mr. P. and his son always requested Thorn, which was pleasing to me. It was always nice to see members actually using their recommended individual to caddy for them.

Thorn appeared to be shy and deficient in confidence in certain caddie situations; that was just his nature.

I believe it was in late August of 2012 that I was approached by Mr. M. P. (Mr. P.'s son, who happened to be a friend of Thorn's father). He told me Thorn's father was in stage IV of colon cancer. He was only forty-nine years of age, and it been discovered during a routine colonoscopy (I believe it was his first one). I was shocked that someone relatively so young had been diagnosed with cancer, much less that it had been discovered in such an advanced stage; he had been given three to six months to live.

I knew that Thorn, like the good and dedicated son that he was, was devastated and longed to make his father's last days as memorable as he possibly could. He was able to obtain the opportunity to play at Oak Hills' famed Championship Course with his dad, as well as entertain him at a Boston Red Sox vs. New York Yankees game at the new Yankee stadium in the Bronx. Soon after these events occurred, school was back in session.

I returned to my home in Florida in mid-October of that year, for another season had come to a close in the upstate. It always gave me such elation to leave New York State.

Around Christmas time of that year, I emailed Mr. M. P. to acquire an update on Thorn's father. I mentioned to him that I dreaded that all the negative news had become history. I was not prepared that the response from Mr. M. P. could possibly be worse than I had anticipated.

Before Thorn's father had passed away (as was expected), his mother had died from a severe health problem.

Thorn appeared in the caddie yard shortly after he had graduated from high school the following June. I approached him to offer my utmost condolences. Physically, he had drastically changed, and I observed the results of everything taking its toll. I speculated that he had dropped about thirty pounds since I had previously seen him the preceding golf season. He was about six foot or six one and tipped the scales at about 130 pounds, as skinny as a rail. He looked terrible, but his spirits were fine.

I proceeded to question him about his future. He stated that he would be attending college in Albany, NY, where his older sister, who had recently graduated from some institution of higher learning, had accepted a job in the area of the state capital. But in the meantime, Thorn and his sister had to find a place for his autistic older brother to live since there was no one remaining from the family who could care for him anymore. How much could an eighteen-year-old endure? It was one of the saddest, if not the saddest moment, of my Caddie Master career.

Melvin

In June of 2003 when I became Caddie Master, I acquired an array of diverse individuals, two of whom were elderly black caddies, Pete and Melvin. They were good, faithful workers and an asset to the program. It appeared they were originally from the southeastern part of the United States and eventually migrated to New York. I hadn't seen either of them for a few years. Then in 2013, they returned to Oak Hill, realizing that it would be a busier place than usual with the PGA Championship coming to town in just a few weeks. Melvin had approached me in the caddie yard in early June inquiring if there were any employment opportunities on the horizon. Melvin, I believe, was approaching the age of seventy. One employee at the country club had informed me that Melvin had a brush with the law, but I disregarded the statement since I'd never had an issue with him in the past. I assured him I would do some research and pass on any information when it became available. I soon found a request for seventy-two bags the next day that would require caddies, both singles and doubles.

I said to him, "There is an outing tomorrow guaranteeing one hundred dollars per bag. I don't believe you can handle a double anymore. Are you interested in caddying single?"

"Aw, thank you, Mr. Joe (he was the only caddie that addressed in that manner). I would greatly appreciate that." And then he stunned me with "You know, Mr. Joe, you are the fairest white man I have ever met."

I never realized he'd been treated poorly in that way; I only tried to live by the Golden Rule.

Doc

There was a caddie (I will call Doc), similar to a dozen others, who were members' sons and therefore grandfathered into the caddie program when I became the Caddie Master in 2003. His attendance was poor, and he did not display much respect for authority. He seemed like your average high school adolescent who appeared to have favored the harder walk in life. I had heard from other caddies that he sometimes fought skirmishes with other students in school. Even though I never questioned him about the accusations, I did believe what I had heard.

Now Doc was an excellent caddie and golfer and came from a golfing family, his father being one of the better amateur golfers in the Greater Rochester area. Often, he would caddy for his dad, his uncle, or one of their friends, usually by request. Apart from that, I don't remember his presence very often in the caddie area.

As time passed, Doc went on to graduate from a prestigious Big Ten university and proceeded on to what appeared to be a promising career. And with the passing of time, Doc matured into a fine gentleman. One day, he even approached me to apologize for his behavior in the past when he was a caddie. He was now a full-time member of Oak Hill CC, and I occasionally conversed with him before or after his round of golf.

Life seemed to be progressing smoothly for Doc when suddenly, in his early to mid-twenties, he was stricken with amyotrophic lateral sclerosis (ALS, also known as Lou Gehrig's disease). I was in total shock when I heard the news from a couple of his caddie friends and refused to believe the severity of the situation until I talked with his uncle at Oak Hill.

What a tragedy! It reminded me of the story of Bruce Edwards, who was Tom Watson's caddie on the PGA Tour (*Caddie for Life: The Bruce Edwards Story* by John Feinstein). Bruce was also a victim of ALS and would eventually succumb to it, but he was in his forties! I had never heard of anyone contracting this deadly disease in their twenties. If there is any consolation here, it was heartwarming to discover some of his fellow caddies, especially R. H. and J. P. K., volunteering and greatly assisting their fellow caddie in his time of dire need. Unfortunately, on October 31, 2019, Doc was called to his final resting place.

I had many good and memorable moments in my career days as Caddie Master at Oak Hill Country Club, but, then again, the tragedies are just as unforgettable.

℞ELATED ℐTORIES

Distinguished Guests

Jay Wright

I had the privilege of caddying for several celebrities, most of whom were athletes. In 2002 (the year before the 85th PGA Championship at Oak Hill CC), the club hosted Coaches vs. Cancer, a charity event held every year at some prestigious golf course in the United States. Some of the coaches and attendants that year included Jim Boeheim, Gary Williams, Jim Calhoun, Dean Smith, Phil Martelli, Bobby Cremins, Jay Wright, Frank Beamer, Geno Auriemma, and ESPN's basketball analyst Jay Bilas.

I was approached by the caddie master at that time (I was employed as the assistant manager of the Golf Service Center then), who inquired if I would caddie for Jay Wright, the head basketball coach at Villanova University who eventually would lead his Villanova Wildcats to the 2016 NCAA Basketball Championship over the North Carolina Tar Heels, 77–74. I believe it was a two-man best-ball tournament. I chose that foursome since Villanova was one of the institutions in the Big East Conference, as was my beloved Syracuse University. As it was brought to my attention, the entry fee was something in the vicinity of $3,500 per person, of which $500 went to Oak Hill CC to cover expenses and the remainder to the V Foundation for Cancer Research, founded by North Carolina State basketball coach and ESPN commentator Jimmy Valvano.

As I recollect, the first round was played on the East Course, walking with caddies, and the second round would be on the West Course with electric carts.

It was a beautiful day, temperatures in the mid-sixties when we began. The foursome had a great time, especially with one of the players identified by the name of "The Shempster" being very comical. I do not remember the other two gentlemen in the foursome, but there was plenty of hilarious entertainment. I don't recall any of the golfers being low handicapped, but I would conclude that Jay Wright was a bogey golfer. After round one was completed, I was standing there with Mr. Wright in front of the Golf Service Center when out of nowhere, Coach Boeheim of Syracuse University appeared. Coach Boeheim approached Coach Wright and inquired about what he scored. Coach Wright responded, "Ninety-eight."

Then Coach Boeheim turned to me and questioned what Coach Wright actually shot on the Championship Course. I answered, "What's it say on the scorecard?" Coach Boeheim again drilled me, and I returned with the same answer. It didn't appear Coach Boeheim was all that convinced with the reply he received.

It seemed there was a bet for dinner that Coach Wright would not break one hundred on the East Course. Well, perhaps the Villanova coach had a mulligan or two. I hadn't kept count or the official score; I was just doing my job. But anyway, for the record, the Coach Wright foursome would eventually be declared the winners of the 2002 Coaches vs. Cancer tournament.

Thruman Thomas

I also caddied for several athletes other than Coach Wright. One day, late in my career at Oak Hill CC, I received a confidential call from the CEO of Paychex, Inc. in Rochester telling me that Thurman Thomas would be golfing on the East Course the next day. I figured I would take the loop, caddying for one of the best running backs ever to don a Buffalo Bills uniform. Well, Mr. Thomas arrived with his personalized bag, which was by no means light for a fifty-plus year-old caddie.

We talked football (obviously), the city of Buffalo, and the Buffalo Bills. I did not question him on the experience of losing four straight Super Bowls since I believed I could logically figure out what his answer would be. I do recall him mentioning that he was a member at the Lake Nona Golf and Country Club in Orlando, Florida.

Thurman Thomas was a true gentleman but not a particularly good golfer. Of the NFL players that have played Oak Hill CC, not too many have fared well, with the exception of two quarterbacks—Mark Rypien (Super Bowl XXVI MVP, Washington Redskins), Jim McMahon (Chicago Bears)—and NFL Coach Dick LeBeau. It was an utmost pleasure to spend that beautiful summer afternoon at Oak Hill CC caddying for Thurman Thomas.

Lindy Ruff

I also had the opportunity to caddy for Lindy Ruff, the longtime coach of the National Hockey League's Buffalo Sabres. He frequently brought along other coaches and players from the team to complete his foursome. After I introduced myself to Coach Ruff, we proceeded to the driving range. While adjusting his clubs on the range to put them in their respective order, I realized something peculiar. I could not help but notice that his driver was right-handed and the remainder of his clubs were left-handed. I didn't question him about the oddity but figured he must have carried that over from his professional hockey-playing days: right-handed slapshot though he was naturally left-handed. We proceeded to the first tee. Here, he hit his driver right-handed and his second shot left-handed. Now the third hole on the East Course is a par three, measuring 214 yards from the tips (the farthest tees from the hole). Not too many golfers who play at Oak Hill East use the back tees except for the pros, the scratch and low-handicap golfers, and the wannabes who believe they can bring the course to its knees.

Coach Ruff and his group were playing the men's tees, which on this day measured 176 yards to an elevated green that sloped off drastically in both the front and the back (a vintage Don Ross signature design). If the golfer was short from the hole, he would be chipping about twenty-five yards to the green; if he was over, the player would have an uphill approach shot through the infamous Oak Hill rough. This hole called for accuracy to be on the green with one's tee shot.

Now remember, the coach only had a right-handed driver. The remainder of his clubs were left-handed. Without hesitation, he glanced at the clubs of the other three players and selected a right-handed iron from one of his guest's bags. Every first shot on a hole had to be right-handed, regardless of the distance. It appeared it was part of his standard operating procedure at the par threes to choose a club of his choice from anyone!

I had a marvelous time with the coach and his foursome. The following year, he arrived with another foursome, and Mr. Ruff inquired if I would be caddying for him. However, I was too consumed with other Caddie Master responsibilities. As a result, the request was denied. I assigned a caddie to him who followed hockey thoroughly and was a Buffalo Sabres fan. I mentioned to the lad about the coach's golf clubs just to familiarize him with the situation. Lindy was a decent golfer, as I remember, nothing spectacular. We always chatted after his round and said our goodbyes as he headed to US Route 90 West back to Buffalo.

Now the following year was a different story. Again, he arrived at Oak Hill CC early on a Tuesday morning. I said hello to him and his entourage at the bag drop. I already had caddies assigned to his group, but his caddie was running a tad late. So I threw the strap of his golf bag over my right shoulder and strolled to the driving range. I was at the practice area with Coach Ruff's golf bag, and while I arranged the golf clubs, I noticed something different about his sticks. Yes, he did have fourteen golf clubs as the maximum permitted by the rules of golf, but unlike in the past, half the clubs were right-handed and the other half were left-handed. I never questioned Coach Ruff about the change. I have two theories of what the reasoning could have been. Either (a) he decided he was sick and tired of his par three routine, or (b) someone called him on it. I concluded it was the latter (according to the rules of golf, he was only permitted to use his own personal golf clubs).

Ron White

Most of the celebrities who played at Oak Hill CC during my time as a Caddie Master were athletes or related to the sporting world, as I had mentioned earlier as the names on the famous Wall of Fame. The one celebrity who wasn't an athlete happened to be a comedian.

He arrived in the parking lot the farthest distance from the clubhouse and found a parking space for his mammoth black bus. This was the longest mode of ground transportation (outside of a train) I had ever seen in my lifetime.

Earlier in the day, I had not recognized this golfer's name on the tee sheet. I questioned the general manager of Oak Hill CC at that time, known as the Ruler, if he was familiar with this gentleman, Ron White. He said he believed the guy was some sort of comedian.

I then phoned my nephew, Josh, who was an honor caddie in the program, and asked him if he would like to caddie at two o'clock that afternoon for this twosome (Ron White and his manager, who were in town for an engagement the following evening).

In the meantime, I was talking with Gene (a lifetime caddie from Secession Golf Club, Beaufort, SC) and asked him if he had ever heard of a comedian named Ron White.

He replied, "Are you kidding me? He is the biggest comic in the southern United States."

Mr. Dyxmit overheard our conversation and asked a younger caddie also from Secession GC if this Ron White could be considered the "Bob Hope of the South."

The younger caddie replied, "Who is Bob Hope?"

I proceeded to the golf cart assigned to Ron White and his manager to check on their bags and clubs. His manager returned from the driving range alone. I introduced myself to welcome him and Mr. White to Oak Hill CC. He told me what an honor it was to play on the East Course and that they were more than grateful for the opportunity to be there.

I then introduced Josh, the caddie, to the players. They shook hands and were off to the first tee. After the round, I approached Josh to get information on how the round progressed. He explained it had been a very entertaining afternoon and that he had been paid handsomely, far exceeding what caddies were usually compensated, including tip. He was also given four tickets for Ron White's show the following night and an invitation to accompany Mr. White and his manager to a local tavern, but unfortunately (or fortunately) he had to decline because he was only eighteen years of age at the time.

About a year or so after Ron White's engagement in Rochester, another lifelong caddie informed me that he had watched the comedian on cable TV the night before. During his show, he mentioned that Oak Hill CC was his favorite golf course and the best he had ever played. With his popularity and being the avid golfer he was, I would conclude that he had played many of the finer courses in America.

Tim McGraw and Faith Hill

On June 11th, 2006, Tim McGraw and Faith Hill were in town to perform a concert the following night. I heard that their manager had approached the Ruler seeking permission for several of their group and crew to play the East Course. It appeared there was a request for five foursomes; the Ruler granted one. This was about 3:00 p.m. Because of the foursome, it was necessary to assign a forecaddie to the group.

B, my top caddie, was given the assignment. Rated as the top caddie at Oak Hill CC (and a longtime LPGA Tour caddie), he was paid very well and also received a complimentary pair of tickets for the show, as were the Caddie Master and other employees on Craig Harmon's staff. It was a great concert, and we were seated about five rows from the stage. Just another perk that came with the position.

Memories from the Golf Course

I heard a variety of stories, most of them believable, about many other celebrities or other golfers from members and guests, but mostly from the caddies. These include such legends as a Super Bowl quarterback and Hall of Famer who consumed a can of beer a hole (eighteen holes, teed off at 9:30 a.m.). Then there were two other NFL players who were asked to leave the Dinosaur BBQ Restaurant in downtown Rochester for…let's phrase it as unprofessional behavior.

Other stories include a golf professional and member of the PGA Tour known to tip waitresses four figures, two NCAA championship coaches from the same university who couldn't appear for a 9:00 a.m. tee time in the Coaches vs. Cancer tournament in 2002 due to "lack of sleep," and so forth. Then there was the story of an NFL coach and two-time Super Bowl champion who was interviewed by the Buffalo Bills organization for seven hours and who, in the end, stated that they just didn't want to fairly compensate this gentleman enough (that was the word from his caddie). This was not difficult to understand if you had been a Buffalo Bills fan following Ralph Wilson all those years. The Bills, at that time, had not had a decent coach since Marv Levy, and that was going back quite a ways, from 1986–1997.

Harmon, Murray, and the Storm

There was an incident at Oak Hill that I vividly remember involving Craig Harmon and a retiree named Murray. Most of the retirees who were employed at the club were not there because the wage was so great but for the benefit of golfing on such a prestigious, historical, and beautiful piece of real estate, even if the privilege only occurred once a week.

There was a severe weather warning in the vicinity of Oak Hill Country Club forecasted for a particular triple-*H* (hot, humid, and hazy) August afternoon in 2007. Our golfing facility possessed one state-of-the-art severe weather warning system to notify any and all golfers on the courses to immediately seek shelter. For some unknown reason, neighboring Irondequoit Country Club's sirens always preceded Oak Hill's; the sound that was emitted was highly discernible for anyone to hear on either of the properties. After the fact, Mr. Harmon appeared in the Golf Service Center to inform Murray to grab a Club Car and drive through the elements to warn the members and whoever else was playing golf to return to the clubhouse as soon as possible for their own safety. At that time, there were multiple flashes of lightning overhead, deafening thunder, and the rain was pouring down ferociously.

Murray vociferously replied, "Are you kidding me? You're paying me eight dollars an hour and want me to risk my life for a bunch of dumb millionaires? Who are the stupid ones here?" Nothing more needed to be mentioned.

Caddie Master Dilemma

Having two exceptional caddies ranked a bit above the rest of the field was a blessing, but in one instance, it became a disaster. There was a member with several big-time Wall Street connections, Mr. S., who requested these two caddies about a week in advance of his golfing date on Oak Hill's famous East Course, together with a couple of other honor caddies. When I informed the gentleman that B and Pappy were already assigned to another member, he requested that I try to persuade the other member to release the two caddies because he had some distinguished VIP guests. When I approached Mr. F. (who was very prominent in the automotive parts industry), with Mr. S.'s request, he stated that his guests were also VIPs from Canada. I left the other member a letter in his locker explaining the situation, but at the same time, I left a negative feeling with the other member. What was I thinking? It should not have come down to this! I mentioned to Mr. S. that although I could not satisfy his request, he would not be disappointed; all the other caddies I had assigned to him were the same classification (honor) as the other two he wanted. There was no money involved for a little extra persuasion with either party. I only did what I had to do to keep the members content.

In reflecting back, what happened was a grave error on my behalf. I never should have gone through with Mr. S.'s request; Mr. F., who originally made the request to have B and Pappy, never should have been approached to surrender the caddies of his choice. I should have just stood my ground and told the awaiting member that his wish would ultimately be denied since the original request for the prime-time caddies would be fulfilled.

In the end, Mr. S., who received four other caddies, was elated. While I was on the Championship Course observing his caddies, everything seemed to be going reasonably well. As I was heading back to the caddie yard in an Oak Hill Club Car, I heard, "Hey, Joe!" Not knowing what to expect, I turned the cart around in the direction of Mr. S. He extended his right fist, raised his thumb, and said two words I'll never forget: "World-class."

After the round, he mentioned that he and his guests were extremely happy and pleased to know that I possessed such a fine caddie program. He paid his caddies handsomely and left with the confidence that I would always have excellent caddies for him and his guests whenever he decided to tee it up at Oak Hill CC.

I felt it was necessary to include this incident since it was the only time in my twelve-year career as Caddie Master that such a situation occurred. The Caddie Master's life was filled with many different experiences.

Jimmy

Then there is the grand story of Mr. Neighbor. I observed this gentleman's name on the tee sheet one day, along with three guests. I inquired about his background from the manager of the Golf Service Center, my friend Mr. Dyxmit. I was familiar with just about every member's name in the Gold Book, but this particular name had me puzzled.

Dyxmit informed me that Mr. Neighbor originally had his start in the munitions industry, but he was presently well-known in the restaurant business. He was out of metropolitan New York, and Dyxmit referred to him as a high-roller. I eventually discovered the reason. Mr. Neighbor owned many five-star dining establishments around the globe, some situated right in New York City. The first time I encountered Mr. Neighbor at Oak Hill Country Club, he was driving a monstrous sports utility vehicle, a General Motors product, perhaps a Tahoe or a Yukon.

I had noticed earlier in the week (as was part of my responsibilities) that this gentleman had requested four single caddies for his foursome in the morning on the East Course and two forecaddies, one for each cart, on the West Course after lunch. You were only required to have one, but he desired for everything to be "top-notch" for his guests.

I observed Mr. Neighbor parked his vehicle not too far from the bag drop area, approximately two hundred feet from the entrance of the pro shop (which was eventually changed to the golf shop; don't ask me why—new generation, I guess). I mentioned to my assigned four honor caddies to follow me, which in caddie intellect is about ten paces behind.

I approached Mr. Neighbor introduced myself, and addressed him, saying, "Good morning, Mr. Neighbor. I have four of the finest caddies you will find anywhere ready to assist you and your guests."

He replied, "Thank you. The name is Jimmy. Just call me Jimmy."

Now in all my years working at Oak Hill—or any other country club for that matter—it was always Mr. and Mrs. Jones, Smith, McMahon, or whatever. I felt very uneasy calling a member by his first name. It even took me a few years to feel comfortable addressing Mr. Harmon as Craig, but then he informed me that he wasn't a member at Oak Hill, just another employee; that was even harder to accept and visualize. It never even entered my mind that was the situation until he personally mentioned it to me.

Getting back to Jimmy. On this particular day, the guests in his foursome included "Doc" Rivers (head coach of the National Basketball Association Boston Celtics at that time) and two ex-professional basketball players, John Starks and Greg Anthony. Jimmy always had guests who were very well-known, whether they were in the world of sports, entertainment, or in the business field.

I know for a fact that Jimmy was very generous to his caddies and to all that served him. He paid his single caddie two hundred dollars each for a single bag, and that was when rates were forty dollars per bag. He also paid his forecaddies two hundred dollars per cart. That was the reason he had the cream of the crop of the caddies when he entertained at Oak Hill CC.

Jimmy took his golf game very seriously. I was not aware of his handicap, but after conversing with many caddies who had the pleasure to caddy for him or for his foursome, the overall consensus was probably around ten. He also had incentives for the caddies if his performance was beyond his expectations. One was a thousand-dollar-bonus per caddie if he had an ace (that is, one shot from the tee box to the hole, which never occurred in my tenure as Caddie Master). Then there was another situation which was more attainable: a fifty-dollar dividend per caddie if Jimmy broke eighty. I know this happened at least once.

As generous as Jimmy was, he was somewhat demanding on his caddies and the Caddie Master. Everything needed to be of the highest quality, especially when it involved the people who were there to serve him and his friends.

Since Jimmy was a very diligent businessman, I was always in contact with Doris, his secretary; she let me know when Jimmy was expected and scheduled to be in Rochester, specifically Oak Hill CC. It was essential to know exactly what he requested for his foursome, as far as arrival time at the club, practice at the range and the other facilities, and expected lunch time, as well as to arrange for the pro shop's permission for his group to tee off during restricted member-only tee times (no guests) usually around 12:30 in the afternoon since the blocked tee times were between 11:00 a.m. and 1:00 p.m.).

As mentioned, everything had to be perfect, and I took that as my responsibility to be assured that what he requested would occur. I always checked with Doris (his secretary) the day before Jimmy's arrival to confirm that nothing had changed, that he still had two tee-time schedules (East in the morning and West in the afternoon), and that his six honor caddies had been assigned.

Jimmy had a variety of the best caddies during the few times he played Oak Hill CC while I was the Caddie Master, and there were stories that accompanied just about every caddie who had the privilege of toting his golf bag.

First there was B and Pappy. Jimmy took a liking to Pappy, even though on occasion their philosophies and theories would clash. Jimmy would have preferred Pappy to always caddy for him, but Pappy felt other honor caddies should have the privilege of carrying

Jimmy's bag, a kind of "share the wealth" mentality. A splendid idea, I agreed, and so it was to become a reality.

I believe the first caddie after the Pappy to personally be Jimmy's boy was Jarhead. Jarhead had been an assistant pro at another private club on the other side of town. He was a nice kid, well-mannered, and he eventually became an architect after graduating from the University of Buffalo and then acquiring his masters from the University of Michigan. In all his years of higher education, he achieved a 4.0 GPA. He had forfeited his career as an assistant pro because, as he stated, there was more satisfaction and income in caddying, and he was correct. There were many caddies with teaching backgrounds on my roster, from other assistant pros, teaching pros, and even a caddie who had won many amateur events, was a member of the Southern Methodist University golf team, and eventually became a teacher at the Hank Haney Golf Academy.

Getting back to Jarhead, Jimmy laced his drive on the first hole, and, being an excellent caddie that he was, Jarhead was waiting at Jimmy's golf ball in the fairway to hit his next shot. When Jimmy finally arrived to proceed with his round, Jarhead had selected a 7 iron for Jimmy's approach shot, just leaning there against the bag.

"Don't ever club me," Jimmy steamed. "Don't think that you know my game!"

That took the wind out of Jarhead's sails, as well as gave a blow to his somewhat super ego.

Well, not too long after that adventure, I believe it was K. O. D. next in line to caddy for Jimmy. Now his father was an ex-NHL player, and so the lad had no problem with discipline. An excellent caddie and golfer, he knew what was expected of him as far as his duties on the golf course. On this particular day, early in the round, Jimmy hit the green in regulation. Like any good caddie, K. O. D. handed Jimmy his putter before retrieving the divot.

"Don't ever hand me the putter until I ask for it!" Jimmy snapped.

Wow! Are you kidding me? What can I say? The caddie was only following standard operating procedure! Isn't that what the professional caddies do on the PGA Tour?

My favorite episode concerning Jimmy and his caddie came at the expense of Nicklo. Nicklo was no stranger to the sport of golf; he was an excellent caddie and a member of the Monroe Community College golf team. At the time of his assignment, Nicklo had just recently some dental work completed which included braces with rubber bands on each side of his mouth. Playing the Championship Course, Jimmy and his three guests arrived at the thirteenth hole. This just happens to be Oak Hill's signature hole, the one you may have seen photographed in many publications about this golf course. It is a long par five, measuring close to six hundred yards from the tips. Most golfers play this hole about forty yards shorter, from the men's tee. From my recollection of how it was explained to me, Jimmy's approach shot, his third was behind the hole (where you definitely don't want to be), about twenty-five feet from the flag.

So Jimmy was now studying his putt, downhill on a well-manicured green that was probably reading around thirteen (I am not aware of ever seeing a reading higher than fifteen, and that was on Augusta National) on the Stimpmeter (an accurate device used to measure the speed of a putt on any given putting surface) with a nasty left to right break. Translation—this green is fast. He then asked Nicklo for his assessment on the situation and to give him a line. Nicklo proceeded to point with his finger to a specific spot on the green, figuring about a three-foot break from left to right. Jimmy bore down to putt, giving serious thought to his golf ball finding its destination. After he stroked the ball, Jimmy sternly stated in disgust, "What kind of a read was that? Are those rubber bands putting a strain on your brain?"

Nicklo was frustrated, and he had every reason to be, for the consensus from the other caddies (all top honor caddies) concluded that Jimmy's attempt wasn't even close to the spot where Nicklo had instructed him to putt the ball and that Jimmy struck the ball with more force than was required. Basically, that's the rule in the game in golf: when something goes wrong, it's always the caddie's fault.

One of Jimmy's biggest assets was his generosity. He paid all his caddies more than anyone at Oak Hill by far. Nobody—and I emphasize nobody—tipped like Jimmy at Oak Hill, or anywhere else for that matter, not even close. I know there are others out there, but not many I have had the privilege to come in contact (with the exception of Joe Namath and Phil Mickelson).

Figure 4: Just a couple of Joes from the Turtle Creek Club in Tequesta, FL (2007).

That brings me to a story the Ruler told me some time ago. It happened at the Inverary Country Club in Lauderhill, Florida, back when it hosted the Jackie Gleason Inverary Classic. For the past eight years or so, it was the home of the Honda Classic, played at the PGA Resort in Palm Beach Gardens, Florida. The host will change in 2025). One day as Jackie Gleason was approaching the clubhouse entrance, a bellboy proceeded to open the door for the famous actor.

At that moment, Mr. Gleason presented the lad with two one-hundred-dollar bills.

"Bet you never got a tip like that for holding the door open," he said, beaming.

"No, sir," the young man answered.

"And what was the biggest tip you ever received for doing that same act of kindness?" Jackie asked.

"One hundred dollars, sir," he replied.

"And who was the cheap son of a bitch that gave you that?" Mr. Gleason inquired.

"That was you, sir, last year."

VWMD

I'd like to share an example of what I meant about frustrations of season-ending play and the lacking number of caddies. It was early October in 2013. It was wetter than usual, and on this particular day, of course, there were no riding carts. Now there was a member, VWMD, who didn't possess the greatest disposition and definitely was not a people person when it came to employees. After the Institutions of Lower Learning, nowadays referred to as colleges and universities, resumed their scholastic year, the caddie program became very limited. In fact, most members or guests who preferred caddies reserved them up to two or three weeks in advance. When I had only, let's say ten to twelve available bodies—and usually no more than eight or nine on any given day—just about all loops were requested in advance.

So here we were on a rainy, no Club Car day at Oak Hill, and VWMD approached me to employ a caddie. Now this was my eleventh year as Caddie Master, and this elderly gentleman had never employed a caddie in his life. To make things more interesting, he was entertaining a guest. And yes, he believed his guest deserved a caddie. Well, lo and behold, he glanced around the caddie yard and noticed four caddies in their caddie bibs.

"I need one of your boys to caddy for my guest," VWMD stated.

To which I replied, "I'm terribly sorry sir, but these caddies are not available. They have been reserved by other members. I only possess a limited number of caddies this time of the year." I expected he would understand the situation.

Unfortunately, being so ignorant of the caddie program and how it operated, his response was "I *demand* you give me a caddie!"

"I apologize, sir, but that is not going to happen." Finally, he rushed to the pro shop in anger. I never did see him again. That, in a nutshell, was the problem. Had VWMD had any knowledge of the system and how it worked, it never would have been an issue. But like I mentioned, I'm sure this member had never taken a caddie in his lifetime, not at Oak Hill Country Club or anywhere else, for that matter

THE MAJORS

The 2003 PGA Championship

In my career as Caddie Master, Oak Hill Country Club would serve as the host of three major golf tournaments: the PGA Championship in 2003, the Senior PGA Championship in 2008 (Champions Tour), and the PGA Championship in 2013. In the golfing world, when any club is the site of a major tournament, that event puts that host country club and the geographical region on the map and brings them to the attention of millions of golf fans worldwide. Of the four golf majors (the Masters, the US Open, the (British) Open, and the PGA Championship), only two annual majors will be held at any venue as selected by the PGA and the USGA (the Professional Golfers' Association and the United States Golf Association, respectively), those being the PGA Championship and the US Open. The Masters is hosted at Augusta National Golf Club in Augusta, Georgia, and the Open is always conducted in Europe, including England, Scotland, and Northern Ireland.

Back in August of 2003, the PGA Championship returned to Oak Hill CC. Although I was the official Caddie Master at Oak Hill CC at the time, that role for this tournament would be handled by volunteers from the membership of the club. Since it was a Major, every contestant had his own personal professional caddie; no other caddies were needed. As a result, and since I had been an assistant manager of the Golf Service Center the previous year, my responsibilities involved the smooth operation of the practice areas and the shuttling of the professional golfers from one location to another.

During the tournament, the West Course became the stage for all the players' preparation. The makeshift driving range stretched from the fairway of the ninth hole to across the seventh fairway. The tee boxes on holes one and ten of the West Course also served as driving ranges. Short game accommodations would be Oak Hill's own practice facility located behind the bleachers of the makeshift driving area, and also the ninth and eighteenth greens would be available for putting purposes on the West Course.

Part of my responsibilities included stocking the tent in the practice area with golf balls for the contestants and clearing the driving ranges (in the caged picker) and practice facilities of golf balls when necessary. Since most professional golfers were under contract to use certain equipment, there were seven different manufacturers of golf balls available: Tiger Woods's personal Nikes, the Nike tour ball, Titleist Pro V (the Titleist Pro V1 and V1x were not available at this time), Hogan, Precept, Taylormade, and Callaway. (Speaking of Mr. Woods and contracts, I remember precisely there were 149 Cadillac Escalades in the main parking reserved for the other professionals and one lone slot for Mr. Woods's Buick.)

Figure 5: Shawn Micheel wins 85th PGA Championship.

Our location was about two hundred and fifty yards from the tee box of the makeshift range to the left. It was not visible to the players or the fans since it was in a heavily wooded area. We were situated under a large tent equipped with coolers, a gas grill, food, beverages, and other amenities, including large flat-screen televisions. Another two hundred yards behind our tent located on the sixth of the West Course, one would discover an area dedicated to manufacturers' trailers and athletic facilities for physical exercise and all types of golf equipment and several instructors to assist the players in "tweaking" their game. The seventh hole was specifically designated as the practice area for this facility.

Outside of the work, there were several moments worth remembering. First was meeting touring pro John Daly as he signed autographs on a collection of golf items that were on display in our tent. Another incident involved shuttling Colin Montgomerie and Ian Woosnam from the practice facilities to the manufacturers' trailers area. I recall Mr. Montgomerie speaking to Mr. Woosnam about the last major, which was the 132nd Open that occurred the previous month (July 2003) at the Royal St. George's Golf Club in Sandwich, England.

"That lucky, bloody chap will never win again," Monty chuckled. He was referring to Ben Curtis. It would be his only Major championship, but he was victorious on three other occasions on the PGA Tour. Mr. Curtis was a 300-1 shot to claim the Claret Jug and was also voted Tour Rookie of the Year in 2003.

Perhaps the most memorable moment of Championship Week occurred inside the tent in our area. We were just standing around cooking hot dogs and hamburgers for the staff when a thunderous ovation could be heard coming from the vicinity of the eighteenth hole on the East Course. It was the final day of the tournament—Sunday—about 6:30 p.m. Shaun Micheel had just placed his 176-yard second shot from the first cut on the left side of the fairway to two inches from the hole! It was one of the greatest shots ever in the history of professional golf. The crowd went absolutely berserk! He would finish winning the 2003 PGA Championship by two strokes over Chad Campbell and three over Tim Clark. They would be the only three golfers to finish under par at the infamous Oak Hill East Course.

2008 Senior PGA Championship

So here we are again, five years later, at the site of the first Senior PGA Championship to be hosted by Oak Hill Country Club. Returning to Rochester from Stuart, Florida, was not a relocation I made by choice every year to remain as the Caddie Master (I did so for employment's sake). It was always the same cold, snowy, wet, windy, damp, raw, and downright ugly weather, to say the least. During this time of the year in upstate New York, this kind of weather is quite typical. We always hoped the weather would change for the better by the last full week in May, though it couldn't possibly get any worse. For the most part, it cooperated. The temperature was rising into the fifties and sixties, and the days were getting longer. The grass was turning green, the thousands of trees at Oak Hill were blooming, and the sunshine returned, somewhat more prevalent than in April.

Luckily for the tournament and the Caddie Master, the month of May also brought a flood of caddies returning to the club since most institutions of higher learning finished their academic years and the students and teachers were arriving back to their summer jobs. Translation—this meant most of my experienced honor caddies were looking for work, along with the dozen or so school instructors taking personal days or just skipping out on their educational responsibilities.

Two weeks before the actual PGA Championship, players begin to appear at Oak Hill CC, not many, of course, because low temperatures at night would be dipping into the thirties on some occasions and daily highs were only in the fifties, sometimes not even escaping the forties. But with about one week remaining until the start of the tournament, other golfers began arriving, more or less due to the fact that time was running out to familiarize themselves with the venue, regardless of the weather and temperature. Besides, they figured they couldn't change either one anyway.

As more contestants appeared for the tournament, the requests for caddies also increased. In order to qualify for this event, one had to be at least fifty years of age or older. A good number of these golfers played sparingly on the regular PGA Tour since the competition was much more intense and the talent far superior than that of the older players; it basically all came down to age. Younger players, especially those in their twenties and thirties, were more physically (and perhaps mentally) prepared than the seniors. As a result, many players in the 69th PGA Senior Championship did not employ personal caddies. The field consisted of over thirty PGA club professionals and other seniors who had qualified.

Seasoned and successful golfers from the PGA usually have professional caddies to assist them. For example, Bernhard Langer (Germany) still employs the same caddie, Terry Holt, he used on the European and the American PGA Tour. However, there are other golfers who insist their caddies remain on the regular PGA Tour instead of following them on the Champions Tour (players over the age of fifty) because the prize money on the regular Tour is so much more lucrative compared to what the Champions Tour could offer. The greatest example of this situation can be found in the book *Caddie for Life: The Bruce Edwards Story* by John Feinstein. Tom Watson's longtime personal caddie, Bruce Edwards, was fervently pressured by Mr. Watson to sign off with him, and he proceeded to caddy for Australian Greg Norman. It appeared to have been a rocky relationship (from what I remember), and Bruce returned to his previous role to work for Mr. Watson from 1992–2003.

There were many other players in this Senior PGA Championship who would call on the services of friends, family members, fellow golfers, or local caddies from Oak Hill CC with knowledge of the course to assist them in their drive to the winner's circle. I was fortunate, as I've previously mentioned, to possess a great squad of my caddies to partake in this memorable tournament. In all, eighteen of the caddies on my roster from 2008 would eventually be called upon to assist the golfers in their quest for the Alfred S. Bourne Trophy, the thirty-six-pound cup awarded to the deserving champion.

From the Caddie Master's perspective, there were many fond memories of seeing the legends of golf performing at Oak Hill Country Club. Unfortunately, one, a caddie—the Irish Legend— left a bitter taste in my mouth.

This Irish Legend to whom I refer was an ex-caddie from the Oak Hill caddie program I had dismissed several years prior. The gentleman had been a career caddie at the club with problems with mind-altering substances for many years. When he left the program, he was in his tenth year of sobriety, so he claimed. But his change in character, attendance, and performance as an honor caddie demonstrated otherwise. It appeared he had totally fallen off the wagon.

About three weeks before the beginning of the tournament, the Irish Legend contacted me via cell phone to say he would be caddying in the upcoming Senior PGA Championship. I explained to him that there was no way in hell I would assign him to anyone, not even a golfer participating in the Pro-Am (usually a charitable event of one Tour pro (Pro) teaming with three or four (usually very wealthy) Amateurs (Am). He informed me that he had been assigned by a Mr. Milkwood, who happened to be the caddie master at an exclusive, prestigious club in Hobe Sound, Florida.

I later discovered that the Irish Legend was a good friend of the caddie master and would be caddying for Mr. D. C. from Jamaica, not during any practice round but on the first day of the actual tournament. Though I should have, I would have never overridden the decision of another caddie master's assignment, especially from a well-established country club, and in a Major championship, no less.

This team of the player and this caddie lasted exactly nine holes! I overheard a conversation in the caddie yard that a caddie had been fired by his player. I had a gut feeling who the caddie involved might have been, and I was correct.

After his competition in the first round had been completed, I encountered Mr. D. C. on the practice green putting. I approached him and apologized for the performance by the Irish Legend. He stated that he should never have trusted the other caddie master's selection; he only wished he had contacted yours truly before the tournament began. In our conversation, I learned that the Irish Legend had given him the wrong club on several occasions and could not read a putt to save his life. Now remember, this caddie had been working on this course at least a thousand times in his career! As a result of his poor performance, the Irish Legend had been replaced by Mr. D.C.'s wife, who also caddied for her husband in the second round. Mr. D. C. claimed after the first round that the Irish Legend had cost him at least six shots to par after only nine holes. In the end, Mr. D. C. missed the cut by four strokes. Ouch!

The tournament in itself was thrilling, to say the least. Saturday and Sunday saw many leaders at different stages of the tournament, including Rochester's own (and an Oak Hill CC member) Jeff Sluman and even the Shark, Greg Norman, making a futile charge on the back nine in Sunday's round. The eventual winner was Jay Haas, with a tally of seven over par. Again, Oak Hill CC, with its unforgivable rough (6–8 inches of double-seeded thickness) and the cool temperatures, had little to no mercy on the contestants. Another upstate New York resident from nearby Horseheads, Joey Sindelar, had a successful tournament, finishing tied for third, two shots behind Mr. Haas. Jeff Sluman would eventually finish at a respectable tie for ninth.

One positive note for the Oak Hill caddie program was that one of our own, C. U. Later, was on the bag of Billy Britton, who, although he finished sixteenth overall, was the low club professional, finishing first in that category of thirty plus of his peers. C. U. Later explained to me after the Championship that while Mr. Britton paid him well, the money meant nothing; it was an honor and privilege just to caddie and participate in a Major, even though it was a senior event. The Rochester community was well-known throughout the golf world for its generous support and huge galleries when a prestigious golf tournament came to town, and this championship would be no different.

Pre-2013 PGA Championship Conditions

The 2013 golf season at Oak Hill CC consisted of an extremely wet summer that resulted in riding carts being banned on the East Coast from June 3rd until the week after the 95th PGA Championship had been completed. Since the Men's Invitational was always scheduled in the first full week in August (the 5th to the 12th), it was necessary to reschedule the men's event to mid-July. The whole season was greatly demanding for the Caddie Master, as requests for caddies went through the roof! Between June 3rd and the start of the fourth Major on the PGA Tour, there were twelve corporate outings, and all of those occurred on the East Course. In all my years at Oak Hill filling the position of the Caddie Master, this was the only time I was satisfied to see pull carts (that is correct—pull carts) at such a prestigious country club.

Obviously, with no riding carts available, the demand for caddies was excessive, numerous times to the point where caddies were no longer available. I carried about sixty full-time caddies on my roster, most of which were able to double. On any given day, I would be ecstatic if 75 percent of them made an appearance to work. I could always count on my friend from the Country Club of Buffalo (Mr. J. G.) to transport about a dozen caddies to assist the Caddie Master in critical situations.

Figure 6: Three of Oak Hill's finest Caddies (practice round - 2013 PGA Championship).

June 3rd was perhaps the first and most important of these out-ings. It consisted of the top brass of the Professional Golfers As-sociation and the defending champion (who happened to be Rory McIlroy) in the first two foursomes. My seven top caddies would carry those bags, all singles. Mr. McIlroy would employ his own personal caddie.

So here I had seven of my best honor caddies, including No More. No More was a school teacher who just happened to call in sick that day so he could caddy in this event. As fate would have it, he was shown on the local television sports news when he was supposed to be teaching! I do not believe anything ever came of it, except for perhaps some nervousness in the next few days.

There were also two other PGA-sponsored outings scheduled later for that particular week. Talk about being tough on the Caddie Master! My daughter and her fiancé (both former employees at Oak Hill CC) decided that would be a good week to get married on San-ibel Island in Florida. It was supposed to be a beach wedding, but it poured all day. Beautiful. Since there was no assistant caddie master at Oak Hill, I used two of my honor caddies, Pappy and Jarhead, to manage the affairs in my absence.

Returning to work was hell—by far the worst three consecutive months at the helm. Everybody and their brother wanted caddies, and many times I was limited. Never had I been in a situation in the past where sixty caddies on my roster could not get me through the summer. And don't forget, there were no Club Cars to be seen anywhere until a few days short of September!

In all my years as Caddie Master, it was heartbreaking to observe the use of carts—supplied by Oak Hill, no less—being used so extensively. They gave the courses an appearance of a glorified "munie." There were sixty of these trolleys located next to the caddie area that were reserved for these two- or three-wheelers. I specifically remember one Saturday in particular when all these contraptions except for one being taken before the good Dr. Nix requested a caddie. Thank God he was one of the few regulars at Oak Hill who always took advantage of the caddie program. Those metal bag carriers were a huge deterrent to the caddie program at a world-class country club of this caliber.

Figure 7: Not the caddie's best friends.

Many of these outings consisted of 144 golfers, many of whom desired caddies. During times like these, it became necessary for me to research sources to fill the gaps. I decided to inquire from my caddies if they had friends or siblings or other relatives they thought might be able to handle caddie responsibilities. In reality, if they could carry a bag, they had a job. It was a huge risk, but for the most part, it proved to be successful. Yes, there were some complaints, but after the situation was explained and logic prevailed, everything operated somewhat smoothly.

I must confess that I had more complaints from these fill-ins than unsatisfied golfers. A couple of these alternates disagreed on what just about every caddie will complain about sometime during the golf season, and that is their wage (what else?). Most of the wannabe caddies did not understand the methods used to determine their pay; they differed depending on the situation. In this case, the outings determined the rate.

Most outings were based on a monetary amount from each player; let's say twenty-five dollars per player. Doing the math, that figure becomes one hundred dollars per foursome. That is only if the caddie was forecaddying. So it becomes the caddie's minimum wage for the round, plus gratuities from each golfer. For the day, the caddie would usually be tipped in the vicinity of twenty to fifty dollars per player, totaling anywhere from $180 to $300, depending on the quality of the job and the generosity of the golfers. The rate was usually determined by the outing committee with input from the general manager of the club and occasionally that of the Caddie Master himself. Now here is where the problem would occur.

As I have stated on several instances, riding carts were not allowed for these outings, so if the caddies were scheduled to carry golf bags, this meant their rate, plus gratuities, would be the sole responsibility of the player (or players) to whom they were employed. Unfortunately, some substitutes had the belief that the club was also responsible for fattening their wallets with a rate similar to forecaddying. As a result, some discussions were not pleasant, and on a couple of occasions, certain individuals were dismissed permanently.

Since it was 2013 and a Major PGA tournament was to be played at Oak Hill CC, everyone who had an opportunity to golf on the Championship Course took full advantage of the situation. Therefore, there were sixteen outings scheduled that golf season. In any other year, the number of these events would be in the seven to ten range. Five of the sixteen outings in 2013 would be sponsored by the PGA of America.

I am not familiar with what the PGA spent on their outings, but I do know that outings are not cheap. Any outing could run in the fifty-thousand-dollar range. I have seen entry gifts for the contestants, including clothing, golf accessories, luggage with the particular Championship's logo emblazoned on it, trips, cruises, you name it. I remember one outing where one hundred players not only received gifts like those mentioned above but also $250 gift certificates in the Oak Hill CC pro shop. I'm sure one individual in the pro shop was extremely happy!

My point is, this was only one country club; these events happened at hundreds, if not thousands, of private country clubs throughout the country. Many of these events are affiliated with health care, insurance, real estate, sports organizations, media, and charities. Think about this next time you pay for some unexplained rate hikes, service fees, executives' salaries and bonuses, etc.

Another thing to consider was that these events were mostly social gatherings rewarding employees and/or clients for their industrial or financial contributions throughout the year. At Oak Hill CC, most of these outings would consist of several "grazing" stations and "watering" holes, plus lunch and dinner (with open bar, of course). On average, it was a ten- to twelve-hour day, with the actual golfing itself (usually a scramble format) taking five and a half to over six hours to complete—and, mind you, this was with caddies! Believe it or not, riding carts or walking with caddies makes absolutely no difference in time finishing a round of golf in these events.

Enough said about the outings; in the end, they are extremely monetarily rewarding to Oak Hill C. C. or any hosting country club, as far as that goes.

Leading up to the PGA Championship itself, there were all types of events and preparations occurring at the club. From the golfing perspective, there were always Men's Special Guest Days (which was a misnomer since there were now full-paying women members), perhaps a dozen in all in 2013. Regardless, about six weeks before the tournament, one was scheduled and full, as would be expected. As I mentioned earlier, in this event, a member could invite three, seven, or eleven guests, at roughly one thousand smackers per foursome.

For the first time in my career at Oak Hill CC as the Caddie Master, Jimmy decided to entertain seven guests for the event. So as Jimmy always requested, I had eight caddies assigned to him and his entourage. On the day prior to the event, I contacted Doris (Jimmy's secretary) to inform her that all the arrangements had been accomplished to keep Jimmy satisfied.

Now on the actual day, Doris called to inform me that Jimmy would be arriving earlier than anticipated because "the boys" wanted to practice. There was only one issue present with that—the driving range was all covered with hospitality tents for the upcoming PGA Championship. I told Doris there was a potential problem. Next thing I know, Jimmy contacts me from his private jet to inform the Caddie Master that he is aware of the situation and has faith in me that I can resolve the problem. He stated that he would be at Oak Hill in an hour. Hmmm…first of all, what were my options? There were three other private country clubs within three or four miles of Oak Hill (two of which accessible by electric carts) where I had good relationships with all the head golf professionals. The thought had entered my mind that surely one of these fine clubs would honor my request. Then I figured there just had to be an easier solution. I proceeded to the pro shop and discussed the situation with Jersey Jeff. He mentioned to me that even though Jimmy had seven guests, he was a member and therefore had the privilege of practicing at Oak Hill C.C. wherever he could find room. I contacted Jimmy on his private jet to remedy the problem. I stated his right as a member, and he was elated.

"Any suggestions, Joe?" he asked.

"Jimmy, all your caddies have been informed and will be ready for you and your guests when you arrive. I would strongly suggest playing holes number one, two, three, and then hike over to number nine on the East Course. The shotgun start is scheduled for 1:00 p.m., so that gives you and your guests two and a half hours to play four holes of practice and enjoy lunch without being hurried. In fact, if you are golfing those holes I recommended, you could add hole number six, a short par three on your way to number nine. That's a total of five holes, consisting of two par threes and no par fives!"

"Great suggestion, Joe," he responded. "Have the caddies ready to go as soon as we arrive."

"I will have the boys stationed at the bag drop upon your arrival. I talked to the starter on the first tee, and you're all set, Jimmy."

"Thanks, Joe; I will see you shortly."

In the end, Jimmy would shell out two thousand dollars on his eight honor caddies and spread his generosity, financially rewarding the Caddie Master as well for his "exemplary service," as he later stated.

Tournament Week

Figure 8: PGA Office (and post 2014 caddie-shack).

Well, the big week had finally arrived. Some touring professionals and other contestants had made their appearance prior to that week, but that was the period of time when the majority of players made their way to the PGA Championship arena. Many of the qualified golfers had just finished competing in the World Golf Championships Bridgestone Invitational at the Firestone Country Club (South) located in Akron, Ohio. The majority of golfers arrived Monday, and the remainder trickled in on Tuesday.

During this time, it was my responsibility to assist the participants with their golf bags to the contestants and caddies registration room. Their equipment would be stored in this area until they had completed their business in the PGA Championship at Oak Hill. This chamber had been converted from the members' health and fitness center of the country club. It would now become the caddie activity center, where the caddies received all the necessary materials for the tournament, plus it also served as their principal dining and socializing area. Their meals consisted of what would be fed to the members and their guests and not to the other employees. This was a considerable difference in the quality of the food and beverages.

As of Monday, the majority of caddies had had not arrived, most of them either driving or carpooling from the previous tournament. Akron was not that far a distance from Rochester, New York, perhaps somewhere around two hundred forty (240) miles, which translated to a four- to five-hour voyage.

Now some caddies on Tour were fairly well off. Those who were fortunate enough to have big-name golfers would, at times, travel with their players (mostly via air) and lodge with them, usually at the residence of a member of the club in the vicinity where a tournament was being hosted. They had little or no worry of being pampered during these events. Other, less fortunate caddies who traveled from town to town in the guise of finding their way to the winner's circle (or a top ten finish anyway) settled for less than ideal conditions. This unfortunately included living on as little finances as possible. In that lifestyle, one would discover, in some instances, ten caddies sharing one hotel room (and not a Ritz-Carlton either), PB and J or baloney sandwiches, cheap snacks and beverages from the nearby supermarket—whatever was the most economical means of survival. These caddies would not spend their money if there was no need to do so.

Take the PGA Championship at Oak Hill, for instance. There was a huge inside room designated for caddies but also an area outside that served the same purpose. Inside, the menu was buffet style, and the quality of the food was what would be expected at a world-class country club, served three times a day, no less. And in the outside caddie yard, one would find four converted vending machines filled with sandwiches, pastries, snacks, fruits, beverages, and so on. These coolers would be totally bare at the end of the day, even while being replenished throughout! These cadies would hoard all the goodies; they refused to purchase anything if it was not absolutely necessary, with the exception of booze, drugs, and tobacco. Don't get me wrong; I'm not insisting that all caddies on Tour act in this manner, but it does happen. As for the regular club caddies, they are not exempt from the ills of society either. If caddie masters had to terminate every caddie with some form of drinking and/or drug problem, it would definitely be a challenge for us maintaining a mature group of quality caddies—for this Caddie Master anyway. Enough said on that subject.

Returning to the Tournament and the players arriving on the scene, I had B and Pappy visible around the main entrance to the clubhouse, just hoping to be noticed as potential and deserving caddies. A few hours passed by when I recognized Mr. Vijay Singh in conversation with B. It was rumored that Vijay went through caddies quickly. From what I had heard, Mr. Singh was extremely demanding and quite impossible to satisfy. It came to my attention that he paid his caddie five thousand dollars a week, regardless of where he finished. It was a very tempting situation—five grand if he didn't make the cut or finished well down the leaderboard. But the intimidating proposition was this: if Mr. Singh won, the caddie would surrender a very lucrative payday. The winner's share in the 2013 PGA Championship was $1,445,000! The rule of the thumb payment for the fortunate caddie was ten percent, I presume after taxes. Anyway, one would have to calculate the caddie rewarded for his labor would be on the north side of one hundred thousand dollars even in New York, which, if not the most heavily taxed state in the country, is close. As I recall, the Oak Hill Caddie, KQ, who caddied for Lee Trevino in the 1968 US Open at Oak Hill Country Club, was paid twenty-three hundred dollars. But let's not forget that was forty-five years ago, when first place in this major golf championship was awarded only thirty-thousand dollars. Boy, how times have changed. (Thank you, Mr. Woods!)

It's totally up to the caddie; either he worked for the guaranteed five thousand dollars for the tournament or hoped for something more lucrative. With the Fijian ranked eighty-two in the world at that time, it appeared his chances were quite slim, given numerous younger and more talented players who had qualified. I'd personally take the guaranteed salary.

From my own conversation with B (after his lengthy meeting with Vijay), I learned no decision had been made. Vijay had inquired into B's caddie experience, to which B answered with his resume on the LPGA Tour, plus his looping at his home course at Oak Hill.

"How many golfers have you caddied for on the LPGA circuit?" Mr. Singh questioned.

"Over twenty," B replied.

"Why so many?" Mr. Singh shot back.

"Because women always change their minds," B quickly responded. Understand, B was well known on the LPGA Tour caddie circuit and spent many years in that position.

In the end, Mr. Singh decided to employ his current putting coach as his caddie, which was not a very educated choice. In one instance, the caddie/putting instructor dictated to Vijay a read on the fourteenth green, in which the ball broke in the opposite direction than his prediction! Mr. Singh was visibly upset. On several other occasions, one had to question where the caddie had positioned himself in relation to the golfer, who was addressing the ball for his next shot. (Unacceptable—How to be a Good Caddie 101). Bad investment, Mr. Singh. He would eventually end in a tie for sixty-eighth place out of seventy-five who survived the cut. I seriously believe (as just about anyone would), that he would have been much wiser in selecting B; I'm not saying that Vijay would have won, but his chances of finishing higher than sixty-eighth would have greatly improved.

Later, on Monday afternoon, my two-star caddies returned to the main entrance of the clubhouse hoping for that special moment to arrive. Time was running thin, and just about all the contestants had registered for the tournament.

Meanwhile I walked out to talk to them as I departed from the caddie registration area. Nothing new had happened, as fate would have it. Suddenly B summoned me over to his location a few yards away from the main entrance door where I had just exited.

"Hey, Joe, can you identify that guy over there?"

Now there were actually two gentlemen about sixty to seventy feet away. "Let me evaluate the situation," I said.

One of them, I assumed, was a caddie and the other was the player. You could not distinguish either of them by their appearance. The gentleman on the left was attired in blue jeans with a unbuttoned long-sleeved plaid shirt, exposing his white T-shirt. His accomplice was dressed in what appeared to be black gym shorts, a T-shirt, and flip-flops for his footwear, comparable to several players. Also, he was very thin-framed, I would estimate around six-foot-two of six-foot-three, and with a full head of unkempt hair.

Then I blurted out, "Bubba Watson." Boy, his appearance was so much different than I expected! I was accustomed to seeing Mr. Watson in his customary buttoned-up golf shirt, dress slacks with razor-sharp creases, neatly polished shoes, and of course, the PING visor; he was one of the best dressed athletes in any sport!

It appeared that Bubba was advancing toward the clubhouse when he was encountered by an employee of the security company that the PGA (I believe) had contracted for the Championship. Many of these security personnel are working for not much more than minimum wage, and many of them are not familiar with Tour golfers. (Rickie Fowler looked as ragged as Mr. Watson when he made his appearance, only he had come a week or so earlier and from a different location than the main clubhouse entrance, and security was scarce at that time).

The two gentlemen and the security official got involved in a discussion that apparently dealt with Bubba's lack of identification and/or the credentials necessary to enter the private club. Security had procedures that had to be followed, and with an event of this magnitude and the number of people involved, no one was exempt. So the PGA office was informed of the situation, and a tournament official resolved the issue. Even though I have the utmost respect for Mr. Watson and felt sorry for this man, the security involved were only doing their job.

There came a time around noon on Tuesday, August 6, when a voice rang out in the registration/caddie area inquiring if anyone knew Tiger's caddie. I responded positively that I indeed knew his caddie, Joe LaCava, and proceeded to the front of the room to discuss the situation with one of the directors. It appeared that the Monroe County Sheriff's Department was interested in the time of Mr. Woods arrival, so they could prepare for the influx of spectators and probable traffic at that time. I found Joe LaCava in the immediate vicinity and explained to him the circumstances of law enforcement. He assured me that Mr. Woods would be arriving at three o'clock. I then met with the officials of both the tournament and security to convey the information they were seeking. Within half a minute, I was on my cell phone to inform my friend and freelance photographer, BT, of Tiger's estimated time of arrival. He was so very thankful and eventually showed his appreciation with several quality 8x10s of some of the contestants.

We approached the beginning of the actual PGA Championship on Thursday, August 8. The crowds were enlarged every day, from the practice rounds beginning on Monday, August 5, to the tournament finale on the Sunday of August 11. Throughout the event, I could be found in the caddie areas, both inside and out, but mostly inside. I engaged in conversation with many of the caddies as well as the golfers, both Tour players and club professionals. What

I discovered, not much to my surprise, was that club professionals brought their sons, daughters, wives, friends, friends of friends, fellow golfers, whoever, to caddy for them in this Major tournament. I would bet not more than a handful or so had ever set foot on Oak Hill property, much less the prestigious East Course. In the end, I'm sorry to mention, Oak Hill caddies had struck out in the attempt of securing a golfer's bag in this venue.

Thursday arrived, and it really had little impact on the Caddie Master. I went about hanging around the caddie areas and spending time on the practice green, just observing the contestants and their caddies. Chat with this one and that one—that's basically how these days went. I wasn't much of a spectator on the golf course itself, just picking up the tidbits of information and activity on the numerous televisions scattered throughout the clubhouse. I did stroll around the course a few times just to engage in conversations, mostly with ex-caddies and people I had come to know in my years as Caddie Master at Oak Hill and, of course, the present caddies who were employed by CBS, Greg Norman enterprises, the PGA, and an assortment of other vendors. It was quite busy, even outside the tournament play itself.

The most eventful day of the tournament (to me, anyway) had to be Friday. It had rained heavily in the morning—a plentiful saturation of the East Course. What accounted for the higher scores in the past Majors at Oak Hill was a combination of slick greens, the six to eight inches of rough, and the numerous hazards on the Championship setting. The precipitation contributed to the course playing somewhat easier, softer and slower greens, resulting in the lower scores. It became similar to a game of darts; just shoot at the target. The greens were holding everything, which was not usually the norm at Oak Hill. By the afternoon this time of the year, the landing areas were firm, and the greens were also lightning fast. This definitely was not the case after the morning storms.

Ben Hogan has held the record of 64 since 1942 on the infamous East Course (it had been tied by Curtis Strange in the 1989

US Open, which was his second consecutive US Open Championship). Earlier on this Friday in the 95th PGA Championship, Webb Simpson also tied the record with a fine 64 himself. Later in the day, Jason Dufner, the eventual winner, would fire a 63 to claim the new course record. It was the first seven under par score ever recorded in a professional tournament at Oak Hill Country Club.

It is my personal belief that two golfers would never equal and/or break the great Ben Hogan's original course record (which he held onto for seventy-one years) on the same day. The two greatest contributing factors were the weather and the technology. It's like comparing baseball to softball—basically the same game but different equipment. One may even conclude the Stone Age vs. the Industrial Revolution. A sixty-three is a great score on any course, and Mr. Dufner deserves credit. But Hogan's sixty-four seventy-one years prior, to me anyway, was a bigger accomplishment. So history proved this golf phenomenon was possible but totally unlikely.

Let's look at the numbers of the 2003 and the 2013 PGA Championships both contested at Oak Hill CC East Course. The 2003 tournament produced exactly three scores under par: the winner Shaun Micheel at -4, runner-up Chad Campbell at -2, and Tim Clark in the third place at 1. In 2013, there were twenty-one golfers under par, led by Jason Dufner at -10. He was seven under in round 2, which translated to -3 the rest of the tournament. In contrast, Webb Simpson was six under par in round 2, but ended the Championship at plus 1; that's seven over par the other three trips around the course. Do the math. Of the twenty-four players who ended at par or better, eighteen did so in the second round.

Finally, the 95th PGA Championship had come to a close, thank God; I was totally exhausted by that time. I even departed from Oak Hill before the tournament was officially over. I received word over the next few days that several employees were partying with some Tour players and their caddies into the wee hours of the morning. I was just so elated it was finished.

It was now Monday following a Major—translated, that meant time to get the course back to somewhat normal. The grounds crew was busy getting the trampled earth back to respectability. It would take months for this to be accomplished. The multitude of tents were being dismantled, carpets torn from their foundations, wooden platforms recycled, chain-link fences rolled up for future use, etc. Employees could get plants, carpet, flowers—whatever vendors did not want or were being discarded on this day. Merchandise was also being offered at prices slashed up to ninety percent!

After some time off for the employees after a grueling three months, the following Monday would get back to a so-called normal life at Oak Hill CC. There were still at least two months remaining in the golf season in upstate New York. The guest lists did not get any smaller (except when a Major Championship was hosted by a particular country club), and there were still a half dozen corporate outings scheduled in the books. On top of that, the prestigious John R. Williams Tournament would be held in mid-September. In the end, I must say, it was relaxing returning to a fifty- to sixty-hour work week.

The Tiger

Three weeks before the start of the tournament, Mr. Woods finally made his appearance at Oak Hill CC without any fanfare. The rumors were so rampant at the club on when this moment would occur. One rumor I specifically remember was that he would present himself at the first tee of the East Course on a particular Wednesday at 6:00 a.m. sharp. The first tee time on any given day is 7:00 a.m., but Tiger is Tiger. So the date arrived, and approximately sixty members were anxiously waiting for that golden moment. The time arrived. As would be expected, it was a no-show, false alarm, whatever you wish to label it.

A few days later, I was loitering around the caddie yard, and I noticed Joe LaCava on his way to the area from the parking lot. I greeted him as he was passing the bag drop area to inquire if I could be of any assistance. He stated that he would like a Club Car for Mr. Woods (he never addressed him as Tiger). Of course, I obliged, and he drove the cart toward the back of the parking lot. He was far enough away when I lost his location in a sea of vehicles.

About half an hour passed, and Mr. LaCava duplicated the same path to the bag drop area he had taken earlier. Again, I said hello and asked if there was any other matter with which I could assist him.

He then smiled and said, "Could I get another Club Car?"

"Sure," I answered but did not inquire why he needed a second cart.

A little while later, I noticed the two carts going in a different direction to the makeshift practice area. This was a secondary area since the main practice area, which stretched from the ninth hole of the West Course through the seventh hole fairway, was not available at that time; it was still under preparation. The first cart was occupied by Mr. Woods and Joe LaCava, the second vehicle by Lindsey Vonn (who at the time was dating Mr. Woods) and one of her sisters. Only the men proceeded to the practice area; I was not aware of the destination of the other cart.

I proceeded to the area where Tiger and Joe LaCava went to practice. Fortunately, there were only a handful of people there (employees), and I just happened to have my camera. The Caddie Master was able to photograph the professional Tour golfer (wearing a pair of neatly pressed khaki shorts, a white golf polo, and a white golf hat while his caddie seemed to be dressed in his working clothes, blue dress shorts, golf shirt, blue windbreaker, blue golf hat, and sunglasses).

Mr. Woods stroked an assortment of irons from this location; it was just a pleasure to witness his unadulterated golf swing. A brief time later (perhaps fifteen to twenty minutes), Mr. Woods and his caddie headed to the first tee of the Championship Course. From what I learned from my caddie, No More (he was in a group with Webb Simpson, Ryan Palmer, and I believe Stewart Cink), the six of them motioned Tiger to hit his tee shot as they awaited just off the first fairway. When Tiger arrived, they asked him if he would like to join the group, thus completing a foursome. Tiger explained he was somewhat in a hurry and requested if he could just play through. It only made sense since Mr. Woods and Mr. LaCava were in a riding cart while the others were walking with caddies. When Tiger had completed his round, he and Joe drove to their automobile and departed. They would not return to Oak Hill CC until the week of the actual tournament.

Figure 9: Mr. Woods and caddie Joe LaCava practicing on a make shift practice area for the 2013 PGA Championship.

The 2013 PGA Championship

Figure 10: Golf Channel's Dave Marr III with the author hoisting the Wanamaker Trophy.

The 2013 season would place Oak Hill Country Club on the golf map again with the 95th PGA Championship. Fans from all over the globe would be flocking to this historic landmark to witness yet another major championship at this prestigious country club. It was golf's final major of the year (which, due to a change in the scheduling of the Majors, is no longer the case), and it would prove to be no disappointment.

There was so much preparation needed for such an event of this magnitude that most people cannot fathom what it entailed. Let's start with the enormous number of volunteers, who were such a great asset to this championship as well as all the other golf tournaments occurring anywhere else in the world. Hundreds upon hundreds of people sought these positions, mostly due to the fact that along with the labor comes the benefits. These usually included free admission to the tournament when they were not working, clothing (volunteers gladly purchased with their own funds since it was only available to them and not the general public), free preferred parking, and the chance to obtain a close-up view of the event and possibly rub shoulders with some of the contestants.

Next, we had all sorts of vendors who were interested in reserving space to sell their merchandise to the massive crowds wanting to purchase their goods. This included all varieties of clothing (PGA, Greg Norman, FootJoy, Peter Millar, etc.), glassware, sunglasses, insect repellent, suntan lotion, sunscreen, camera batteries, food and beverage, and so on. About the only thing I observed sold in past tournaments at Oak Hill CC (and I am going back a ways) that I didn't see present here were the old Kodak periscopes. Believe me, the vendors were recipients of huge profits on their merchandise for the reason they could charge exuberant prices for their wares due to the simple economic condition known as supply and demand.

As far as the clothing aspects went, if I remember correctly, Oak Hill CC was restricted from selling their clothing at this tournament because it was a PGA-sponsored event, therefore the PGA was monopolizing the market. The truth of the matter was much like the 2003 PGA Championship—the Oak Hill CC logo was much more popular than the one the PGA used, which was dramatically demonstrated in the number of sales. This year in particular, the PGA logo used was too large and gaudy. I remember being told by an assistant pro that $40K worth of golf shirts was being returned for the simple fact they were not selling. No one was purchasing them! And this was about a month before the start of the tournament. Also, I don't recall how it occurred, but there was the original Oak Hill logo, which consisted of two leaves and one acorn, which was eventually replaced by another logo with an enormous lettering of PGA Championship 2013 with the Wanamaker Cup above it with two pennant flags on each side. Not too many people were elated by the switch. To me and others, it was the club versus the PGA; why would anyone be surprised by the outcome?

Figure 11: Hats of Oak Hill and PGA Championship logos.

When one arrived as a spectator, this person had to be awestruck at the number of tents throughout the area. It appeared like a Barnum & Bailey circus. There were tents on the range, at both courses, and along the first hole of the East Course. There were hospitality tents scattered throughout and media tents, merchandise tents, food and beverage tents—just tents all over the place! If there was any space to erect a tent, one would be located there. All the flooring in these tents were cheaply carpeted and decorated with plants and flower arrangements. So on the day following the tournament, one would observe employees and others helping themselves, with the blessings of the vendors, to the carpeting, the vegetation, and floral displays. Even the PGA of America and Oak Hill CC fence coverings were cut and rolled up in sections and carted away as souvenirs. (I personally was able to acquire about an eight by twelve-foot section of this covering with both the 2013 PGA Championship and Oak Hill CC logos, which are now folded in my desk. Unfortunately, that desk was located in the basement area that was shared with the new golf shop personnel. Case closed). Leftover goods from several of the vendors could be found with discounts up to 90% off. To those who took advantage of the situation, it was perhaps considered the best day of the tournament (for employees, anyway).

Television coverage also had a very active schedule in preparation for this event. A week or so before the tournament, there is what they refer to in the golf world as the flyover. You can observe this on the television where golf fans get a bird's-eye view of the topography of the playing field (the East Course). In this event, a cameraman in a helicopter would film the Championship Course from the air to educate the people on the terrain of this real estate. This would provide one with the knowledge beneficial as with club selection, hole location, yardages, and strategies used in certain situations. During a flyover, you will never see any person, vehicles, machinery, or equipment that would steal from the natural beauty of the golf course. You will notice this any time you view a flyover at any country club hosting a major or other prestigious golf event on the television or on any video device.

Caddies During the 2013 PGA Championship

Now even in this time where the PGA Tour Players relied on their own personal caddies, a select group of Oak Hill CC caddies still possessed the feeling that at least one of them would be lucky to loop in the tournament. After a couple members on the Caddie Committee for the event conferred, it was suggested we establish a ranking system with the top ten caddies selected in the program. There were several minor disagreements (as I had expected), but nobody knew the caddies as well as the Caddie Master. I'm sorry, but unlike some members, I would not embrace any bias in my rankings. They knew who appeared to be the best choices, but some members on the Caddie Committee allowed personal feelings and commitments to play a role in some of their positionings of the caddies. I recorded all the ratings of every caddie, and I was fair, as just about every caddie would attest. My knowledge of the caddies at Oak Hill CC was second to no one.

I still figured I'd be fortunate to get two or three of my honor caddies in the tournament. I specifically remember Jarhead (an ex-assistant pro from another private country club located crosstown) expressing that he would be greatly disappointed if he didn't get a loop. Unfortunately, we had him rated number eight in the top ten. I knew from experience what disappointment could be about, but it was nothing compared to my personal devastation at the 1968 US Open. Anyway, my two top loopers, B and Pappy, were hanging around the main entrance of the clubhouse, hoping to be noticed by a contestant who might just be in need of an excellent veteran caddie. I cannot recall who B caddied for in the practice rounds leading up to the tournament, but I do know for a fact that Pappy caddied for Stewart Cink three straight days, and Mr. Cink was truly appreciative of Pappy's work ethic and overall knowledge of the game, caddying, and the golf course.

The earliest of the well-known participants to arrive at Oak Hill Country Club were Ryan Palmer and Webb Simpson, and both employed Oak Hill caddies in their practice play. Even though they gave excellent reports on their respective caddies, they both employed their own personal caddies for the Championship, which was totally expected; anything else would have been shocking.

There were other touring pros who appeared as the time to the start of the Championship approached. The golfer I vividly recall meeting at the bag drop was Rickie Fowler. I was mildly set back when he arrived wearing gym shorts and a T-shirt—not what I had expected. I proceeded to escort him to Craig Harmon's office; they all knew Craig and the Harmon family. Anyway, about twenty minutes later, Mr. Fowler was observed having a putting contest with a group of members' children who had assembled to get a glimpse of their hero. Such a fine gentleman—smiling, signing autographs, and distributing his infamous orange Puma golf hats. He was a great ambassador for golf and the PGA Tour, as well as a status symbol of the younger generation. Such a real class act!

So within an hour after Mr. Fowler headed to the first hole for a taste of Oak Hill's East course, Phil "Lefty" Mickelson made his entrance, smiling from one ear to the other, and headed up to the pro shop to say hello to Craig. On his way to Mr. Harmon's office, he handed the assistant manager of the Golf Service Center a $100 bone for his crew. What a nice gesture! Believe me, not many, if any, of the touring pros followed suit.

Hard to believe, but most of the professional golfers wore khaki shorts and a collared golf shirt as their attire while practicing for the Fourth Major. There were several who donned a pair of slacks, but I noticed the slight majority of the contestants wearing shorts as opposed to golf slacks.

Mr. Mickelson descended from the pro shop about half an hour later and was headed toward the first tee with Bones (Jim Mackay), his caddie of twenty plus years. Also, per his request, he had one security personnel and no media in his group. On his journey to the East Course, he encountered a swarm of young kids, autograph seekers. He signed a few and then addressed the crowd, saying, "It's time to go to work. That course is my office. I will see you later when I have finished my business." So, he proceeded onward to the first tee with his caddie to tackle the monstrous Championship Course.

In the meantime, I returned to the designated caddie area, just adjacent to the Golf Service Center. I was in a conversation with caddies, a mixture of some Oak Hill boys and some Tour caddies. I observed in the distance an individual headed to the first tee, and I had a hunch he was a Tour caddie. Caddie Masters acquired a sense over the years so he could conclude, just by looks and mannerisms, if someone were a professional caddie. So even though I knew he was at Oak Hill CC to caddy in the Championship, I couldn't readily identify him. Following at a short distance, I noticed his attire of blue shorts, a golf shirt, and hat; and he was somewhat stocky in build.

I approached him from behind and said, "Excuse me, you must be caddying in the Championship. And for whom will you be working?" I questioned.

"Mr. Woods" was his answer.

"So you must be Joe LaCava," I answered as I extended my right hand to introduce myself. "I am Joe Schmerbeck, the Caddie Master at Oak Hill. What a pleasure it is to meet you. On your way to the East Course?"

"Yes, sir," he replied.

"Mind if I join you? There have been a few changes here on the East course that I would like to bring to your attention since 2003." (the last time OHCC hosted the 85th PGA Championship).

"Sure," he said.

So on our way we went, walking on the cart path past the eighteenth hole of the West course, past the eighteenth green on the East, and to our destination, the first hole of the Championship Course. On the way, we have a friendly chat, covering Mr. LaCava's hometown of Newtown, Connecticut, known unfortunately as the site of the massive carnage of twenty-six innocent lives at the Sandy Hook Elementary School in 2012. This terrifying event was not mentioned in our conversation; I had no interest in discussing it with him, and I was positive he had heard enough of the terrible ordeal. I had happened to be in Newtown on several occasions to participate in the Men's Invitational at Newtown Country Club. My brother-in-law was a member at the club, and it was a real pleasure to partner with him in this annual event. But what this private club prided itself was that Freddie Couples's ex Tour caddie was a member there, and that was our mutual connection with Newtown.

We finally arrived at the first hole. Joe LaCava was there to walk the course hole by hole (obviously, I didn't have the privilege to accompany him since my time was limited and I had other commitments, particularly my job). I described to him the changes that had occurred in the past few years—lengthening the tees on several holes, the redesigning of the greens on holes number five and six, and the restructuring of the par three on number fifteen, just to mention the most drastic of all the changes.

For those not familiar with the East Course at Oak Hill CC, the first tee area is in the shape of a large perpendicular **L** The long part of the **L** is the first tee, and it shares the tee area of the fourteenth hole (the bottom part of the **L**), but the tee locations do not interfere with one another. As Joe LaCava and I were discussing the first hole, from the upper tee area, "Bones" Mackay (his long-time caddie) joined us to say hello. So there stood the three of us while Mr. Mickelson could be found on the fourteenth tee, practicing. That particular hole was listed as a 323-yard par four. It appeared that Lefty was attempting to locate a landing area for his first shot in order to have a flat lie for his approach to the green. Again, it was only 323 yards, but from about 260 yards out to the green is all up-hill; therefore, positioning the tee shot that hole was of the utmost importance. It was drivable for many of the golfers at that time, but the green was heavily guarded by two huge sand traps, one on the left and one on the right, and in between the two, one would find the legendary Oak Hill rough. In my opinion, it was quite a gamble and really not worth the effort because if the drive cleared the green, there was a fair possibility the golfer could discover he was out of bounds in Oak Hill CC's neighboring Irondequoit Country Club.

Anyway, the three of us were standing on the first tee, and a voice from the fourteenth tee, speaking with some volume, said, "Hey, Joe." Bones nudged me and stated that Mr. Mickelson was addressing yours truly (and not Mr. LaCava). Kind of stunned, I walked over as Lefty extended his right arm toward me and introduced himself.

"Hi, Joe. I'm Phil Mickelson. No kidding. "I heard you have a great caddie program here."

"Thank you, Mr. Mickelson," I replied. "And I would like to thank you personally for all you have done for golf and the caddies."

I had recently read an article from *Golf World* or some other golfing publication prior to this event that on occasion, Phil Mickelson would take a large number of Tour caddies out for dinner and then leave the servers a four-figure tip! It was not really surprising—I had heard that Mr. Mickelson was a very generous individual indeed!

I was truly taken aback when Phil Mickelson mentioned to me that there was a consensus that I possessed a great caddie program at Oak Hill CC. My question was where had he heard that? I was not quite positive how information on caddie programs traveled, but I do recall the times (probably close to one hundred) in my career as Caddie Master that golf-course raters (usually from *Golf Digest*, *Golf Magazine*, *Golf World*, and other publications) would golf at Oak Hill for the purpose of ranking the facility in comparison to other venues. It is obvious that not only did they rate the golf courses (mostly the East Course), but I would imagine there were several other categories of interest on those reports.

These course raters would generally tee off on the first available tee time, which was 7:00 a.m., with a caddie required. In the course of the day, they would first meet Craig Harmon, then register in the pro shop, visit the locker room, get a cup of coffee, golf, shower, probably have lunch, and visit the Oak Hill CC Museum and then depart. That round of golf would be beneficial to the rater, his employer, the caddie program and Oak Hill CC itself.

There are members who play golf all around the world and compare the caddies from other clubs with the caddies from Oak Hill. After six years in the position of Caddie Master, the program finally came to the point where I was 100 percent confident in the quality of the work provided by the caddies. It paid off, and it was so rewarding when any caddie could loop for anyone without any worry of receiving negative reports. I never received any feedback that other programs were superior, but I would imagine there may have been some bias involved.

As for the PGA Tour, this was a different story. These players would be interested in what a country club of this caliber had to offer. I realize there was plenty of conversation among these golfers, and many used Oak Hill caddies in the past. Also, they all were familiar with the Harmon family, and Craig had been the head professional (as well as an icon) at Oak Hill CC for over forty years when the PGA Championship occurred in 2013.

Remember also, as I mentioned early in the book, that Oak Hill CC was rated as the number one private country club in the nation (in 2010, according to *Golf World* magazine), and the caddie program was also very highly rated. In essence, I would believe that a combination of all the factors involved resulted in Mr. Mickelson's saying what he did about the caddie program at Oak Hill C.C.

It was time to return to Phil's practice round. He stated that he would like to see me at the conclusion. In the meantime, Joe LaCava headed down the first fairway, Bones returned to his caddying duties, and I ambled back to the caddie area.

Just a little bit over an hour passed, and Mr. Mickelson and Bones were headed back toward the putting green, where they were greeted by a huge entourage of fans, mostly children of Oak Hill CC members. Parents were busy clicking photographs while Lefty was happily signing autographs, just as he had promised before he departed for his practice round several hours earlier.

Then Mr. Mickelson traveled back toward the parking lot, still signing autographs as he walked slowly. His location was now in the vicinity of the caddie area (probably about seventy to eighty yards from the practice green) when a woman approached him and requested a photograph of Phil with her son. Now Lefty heartily honored her request, but there stood another small problem. There was a multitude of other parents in the immediate area with the same request. There were perhaps twenty kids present, and Mr. Mickelson had an engagement scheduled in half an hour. After quieting the crowd, he informed them of his situation.

"Why don't we get all the kids together with me, and everyone can take their pictures?" he suggested.

Great idea! Phil extended his arms around all the children gathered together, like a mother hen protecting her young chicks, smiling like everyone else, and all were happy. A photograph with Phil Mickelson was now a prized possession. On July 21 2013, Phil won the coveted Claret Jug at Muirfield Golf Links in Scotland, his fifth Major and his first (British) Open victory. Luckily, I was able to get his signature on the Oak Hill Wall of Fame before his exit from the club. He then thanked everyone and readied himself for his next destination

He approached me, shook my hand again, and stated, "Thank you, Joe; nice to meet you." He extended his other hand to me, which contained a one hundred-dollar bill! Life goes on! There wasn't anyone on the PGA Tour in the same realm with Phil Mickelson. I have had the privilege of meeting many fine Tour players, but no one possessed the charisma of Phil Mickelson. What a class act.

Figure 12: Phil Mickelson's The Open Victory.

Oak Hill CC Caddie Program Rating

I never knew for sure what constituted the ranking of the Oak Hill's caddie program, nor did I ever Google it or do any research on the subject, but other people in the golf world must have possessed information I was not aware existed at the time. I am referring specifically to many cell phone calls and emails on the creation of an excellent caddie program from several golf personnel, both domestic and foreign.

The first offer occurred in 2005 when I received a call from the Westhampton Country Club, located on Long Island, New York. I was offered a job there as the head caddie master with housing and other perks. The problem was the location—New York. That said enough right there. Besides, I believed my caddie program at Oak Hill was still in its infancy stage.

The next incident happened in 2006 when I received a call from a Mr. G. S. representing Caddie Services Inc. (CSI) in Jacksonville Beach, Florida, wondering if I was interested in departing from my caddie master position at Oak Hill CC for the sole purpose of joining their organization. Their offering was not that generous, and a negative response was imminent. Besides, I had just relocated from Rochester to Stuart, Florida, and the caddie program at Oak Hill was still short of my personal standards.

Perhaps the most important call I received concerning my caddie program came to me in the winter of 2009 while I was located at my southern residence. I can't recall to whom I was communicating, but it appeared to be someone in a management position at a highly prestigious country club in Dallas, Texas. We were in a heavy and detailed discussion on the components of a successful and quality caddie organization. We covered everything, including training, recruiting, termination, payment, gratuities, caddie rules and restrictions, dress code, etc. I spoke with the gentleman for forty-five minutes! What was I doing? I didn't realize until our conversation had ended that I did all this for free! Had I not been so stupid and naïve, I should have scheduled a meeting for, let's say, a week and charged their club $10K or so for my expertise! What a dummy!

It is my belief the saddest call I ever received relating to caddies and caddie programs came from a private links club out of Ireland. It was not a single incident that occurred that had the golf manager concerned but rather a great social problem, that being the epidemic of alcoholism. Yes, we spent some time discussing what characterizes a somewhat good caddie program, but it's not achievable when certain elements are lacking. The lad mentioned to me that a number of golfers at the establishment had to resort to caddying since their membership had to be revoked due to lack of finances from their once successful livelihoods. Alcohol has destroyed so many lives and families in the world, but it appeared to be such a problem in Ireland.

Caddie Duties

In preparing for the actual PGA Championship, I was approached by several businesses looking for workers to assist them in their upcoming hour of need. The largest request was submitted by CBS Television, and there was a similar appeal from Turner Network Television (TNT). TNT aired segments of the first two rounds, and CBS carried the final two rounds on the weekend. CBS was, by far, the largest employer of the Oak Hill CC caddies, with more than one half of my older and mature caddies employed by the television networks. It was my understanding that the Communications Workers of America (CWA) was madly bent out of shape when CBS decided to go with workers outside of the CWA. It was obviously a matter of the bottom line, where CBS would pay the scab caddies something like $32 per hour plus overtime (at 1.5x rate) and meals. Union pay was substantially higher plus health care, 401K, and other benefits that would have to be honored had a contract been negotiated. The savings to CBS would be quite substantial. In the end, CBS was happy, the caddies were happy, and the Caddie Master was happy for acquiring for his caddies an honest reprieve from looping. CBS also did the same for the 2003 PGA Championship at Oak Hill CC.

Now these caddies were employed anywhere from sixty to eighty plus hours a week, and perhaps a handful of them worked up to three weeks. At a rate of over $32/hour and $48/hour after forty hours, the money was undoubtedly accumulating. But some of these caddies were in for a tremendous shock. I recalled one of my career caddies (who also caddied at the Country Club of Rochester) pulling me aside and vigorously complaining that he had lost over nine hundred dollars.

"What do you mean you *lost* over nine hundred dollars?" I questioned.

"They took out taxes—over $900!" he explained.

To this, I replied, "Welcome to the real world and living in New York State!"

2013 Men's Invitational

The 2013 Men's Invitational

All the Men's Invitationals at Oak Hill CC were extremely busy and chaotic, and the 2013 Men's Invitational was by far the most hectic, due to the fact that electric riding carts would not be allowed in this event. Talk about putting a strain on the Caddie Master! Let me describe for you what transpired at this tournament.

First of all, there were two golf courses featuring 288 participants. There were eighteen flights, sixteen flights for members/guests under the age of fifty and two flights dedicated to senior members and their guests over fifty years of age). Each team played every other team in their respective flight once for a total of seven matches over three days (Thursday, Friday, Saturday). Depending on their schedules, a team would either partake in two matches on two days and three on the other, or three matches on two days and one on the remaining day. Scheduling was very complex, and in the end, there was the Shootout, with all sixteen flight winners in regular competition and a two-flight senior Shootout to determine the eventual winners.

The first matches of the tournament began at 7:30 a.m. on Thursday. There were seventy-two teams and two courses, eighteen holes each time. Two teams times two people per team equaled 144 players at each Shotgun start. The other three tee times were at 10:30 a.m., 1:30 p.m., and 4:30 p.m.). Friday had the same setup, and Saturday's tee times were at 7:30 a.m. and 10:30 a.m. The teams would play once or twice on Saturday depending on their schedule. Then after lunch was consumed following the last round, the Shootout would commence, usually around one o'clock in the afternoon, beginning on the tenth hole of the East Course. Typically the outcome would be decided by the fourteenth or fifteenth hole.

The Shootout usually started with four foursomes from the sixteen regular flights (the senior flights were separate) with the low score on the hole and ties advancing. When the remaining three teams in the foursome were eliminated, the winner would proceed against the winners in the other three foursomes. The final foursome consisted of the winners in the flight playoff segment of the Shootout, which would yield the overall Men's Invitational champion.

Preparation for the Men's Invitational is a long and tedious process. Since more than 144 teams submit applications, there is a process of elimination. Many factors are involved, including a team sacrificing not to participate one year with a guarantee that they will be playing in the following three (or more) consecutive Men's Invitationals in the future. If I remember correctly, the applications were required to be received by the tournament committee before the beginning of the golf season, perhaps in March of the competing year.

It was in April of 2013 (just like every other year); I returned to Oak Hill Country Club early in the month to lay down an itinerary for the upcoming season. Opening days for both men and women (women on the first Wednesday of May, the men on the first Thursday), corporate outings, the Silver Foils, usually a district event, the Women's and Men's Invitationals, perhaps the League of the Iroquois annual tournament, the prestigious John R. Williams Tournament, and, of course, the 95th PGA Championship would comprise an interesting season.

Getting back to the Men's Invitational, requests would be forwarded for caddies to work in the tournament as soon as I had returned from my home in Florida. Unfortunately, no more than a handful would be employed in the Women's Invitational; there seemed to be a sense of discomfort in this situation at Oak Hill CC. Many of the teams requested the same caddie (or caddies) year after year. In many cases, it was something of a second father relationship. Members who partook in using the caddie organization, not just in the Invitational, would request the same caddies always; that was the main reason these friendships thrived. Eventually, it would become part of my responsibility to guarantee that the respective caddies were available and assigned to the member for future engagements.

Participants in the 2013 Men's Invitational had an inclination to hire caddies due to the PGA Championship being played there and the unusually wet weather. The caddie numbers had become exhausted by early June, and I found myself constantly on the cell phone, daily contacting other caddie programs (locally there was only one, and not a very good one at that), ex-caddies, friends of caddies, and so on, attempting to fill the huge volume of requests for their services.

Every year, the Men's Invitational Committee would furnish the Caddie Master with the master schedule, and, I, in return, would construct a chart (and copies) with all the relevant information. These would be posted in four different locations in and around the caddie area so the caddies would have access to all the facts relating to the event. The charts consisted of the players' names, caddies' names, flight number, tee times, opponents, hole location, course assignment (East or West), points per round, and a running number of points overall for the tournament. Being old-school, all this information was calculated and generated without any assistance from a computer, which didn't bother me a bit. Computers, to me, were extremely frustrating, as it appeared I was always a step ahead of Watson. The club never offered a computer to assist me in my daily chores such as attendance, accumulated points, assignments, vacations, caddie requests, etc. anyway. How times have changed; man no longer has to think for himself.

Twelve hours a day at Oak Hill was the norm for this hectic week of the calendar year but especially this year with the absence of golf carts. It was the only time in my thirteen years at Oak Hill CC that I disregarded my complete dissatisfaction with push/pull carts. Sorry to say, but for all those who prefer to use the trolleys, these contraptions just have no place at a private country club; they are poor substitutes for a caddie. I firmly believe in most cases, it comes down to price.

A few things I failed to mention about this annual event. First of all, one of the biggest happenings of this week was the Calcutta. This was where individuals and/or teams wagered cash on themselves or others to win, place or show, just like horse racing. At this particular country club, thousands and thousands of dollars were bet on teams to win the Men's Invitational. I've read that amateurs would lose their status by participating or accepting monetary rewards for their involvement. I personally have never heard of this occurring, even though the practice is highly disapproved (so they say) by the United States Golf Association (USGA).

Secondly, many of the guests were from out of town and eliminated the complete week from their busy work schedules. After all, for some of these golfers, this was the highlight of their year. They golfed perhaps six or seven days of that week. And, of course, Wednesday was when the activities actually began. This was Men's Stag Day. Lunch was served before the big 1:00 p.m. Shotgun, which consisted of two foursomes on every single hole on both the East and West courses (that is 288 golfers; just do the math!) with beverage and grazing stations throughout. I concluded that in my years as Caddie Master, this was the official commencement of a four-day happy hour.

As for the actual Invitational beginning Thursday at 7:30 a.m., members and guests began arriving at 6:00 a.m. or earlier. Obviously, the employees had been there much sooner, especially those associated with food and beverages. Continental breakfast would be offered every day starting at 6:00 a.m. together with a significant bar area staffed with Oak Hill's finest bartenders, offering mostly vodka wedges, transfusions, and the old standard Bloody Marys. This was breakfast for some members and their guests, even though others decided to partake in the breakfast sandwiches and assorted pastries and bagels. Some players actually insisted on having orange juice and/or coffee with their meal instead of alcohol! Throughout my years associated with this event, I knew three or four members had early parties before the official start because some of them needed alcohol in their systems in order to be able to perform (play golf). Of the four country clubs where I was employed (the other three being in Florida), no other club could compete with Oak Hill when it came to celebrating. Yes, these people were here for a good time, so why not?

Outside of the breakfast, the range and the practice areas were overwhelmed with waiting lines at most practice tees (usually between twenty-five and thirty stations). This year, with the absence of the electric riding carts, which I cannot emphasize enough, there were more bodies around, largely due to the number of caddies being employed. It was no picnic for the Caddie Master. Trying to satisfy requests for over one hundred fifty caddies when I never had requests for more than sixty in any other year was an insurmountable task.

Many caddies fared extremely well financially in that year's Invitational. True, they were committed to seven of the fourteen Shotgun tee times with their respective teams, but this left seven other opportunities where their services could be requested by other teams. Although they were not required to do so nor would they be reprimanded for refusing, many caddies took advantage of the situation. Remember, these were only nine-hole matches, but this event, for the most part, was more monetarily beneficial than a normal day at the club. It was hectic and, at times, embarrassing to plead with caddies to work an extra nine, eighteen, or even twenty-seven holes in addition to their scheduled appointments. Fortunately, I had many caddies who were grateful for their jobs, the money, the golfers, and even the Caddie Master. It was an absolute necessity to have a good and honest working relationship with my caddies and a sense of respect for everyone involved.

These were an exciting three days for most of the people in the tournament, not only for the players but also for the caddies and all the workers in the clubhouse. All flights were closely observed, including who was moving up and who wasn't. Some flights would have teams that appeared to be unbeatable while others were lucky to get a point or two here or there. This was the exception to the rule, that is, the part about a team running away with their flight. I would say that at least half of all flight champions were determined on Saturday, usually in their last scheduled match.

Which brings us to the Shootout—oh yes, the Saturday after-noon classic. Every year, except for 2013, every available riding golf cart could be found on the East Course, with the majority of these vehicles located off the back of the green of the amphitheater-like signature thirteenth hole. Spectators were all over the playoff holes; as mentioned, no carts were permitted in the Invitational, thanks to the wet grounds and the upcoming PGA Championship.

The tenth tee of the East Course became the focal point of the start of the Shootout with the winner of the twenty flights. Usually, by the end of the thirteenth hole, the elements have taken their toll on most teams, with perhaps only a handful or less advancing to hole number fourteen. In my thirteen years at Oak Hill CC, I recall the eventual champions never proceeding farther than the fifteenth hole. With twenty teams, it all comes down to endurance, luck, or both.

I will never forget this one incident on the thirteenth hole of the 2013 Men's Invitational Shootout. There happened to be a team from one of the better flights with one of my honor caddies at the helm who was known simply as the Wizard. This team consisted of two low-handicap golfers. I believe the member was still alive on the hole while his partner had faded (too many strokes), picked up, and was therefore out of contention for the remainder of number thirteen. The member was lying four on this par five, about twenty feet past the cup. (His partner was lying five or six and not yet on the green, that being the reason for taking himself out of contention). Now the member only had to get down in two to advance. The only problem was his position—twenty feet behind the hole, putting downhill on this slick green, and at 4:30 in the afternoon, this green was baked and probably running 13.5 or 14 on the Stimpmeter (in other words, lightning fast). So he sought the Wizard's advice; the caddie responded, due to the quickness of the green, the member only needed to touch it and get it close to his target for a two-putt bogey. The player, wobbling to the ball, stroked it about thirty feet past the hole, resulting with the Titleist rolling off the green! Unfortunately, he was unable to sink the ensuing putt and were therefore eliminated from the championship round.

So I approached the Wizard later in the caddie yard to get an explanation on the circumstances on the thirteenth green. As I assumed, he revealed the story to me exactly as I had written. Alcohol was definitely the deciding factor. In fact, the Wizard mentioned to me that one of his caddie responsibilities on this day was standing and steadying this golfer on the thirteenth tee. Amazingly, it was a beautiful drive right down the middle of the fairway. But, like I mentioned earlier, some of these participants started imbibing early in the morning, and unfortunately, it finally took its toll. The Men's Invitational again lived up to its annual reputation as the Summer Classic at Oak Hill CC.

So the eventual Shootout Champions would rightfully win bragging rights for the next year and collect some very nice prizes and merchandise, but the biggest winners were the ones who bought the winning team in the Calcutta; ask anyone.

2013—The Biggest Moment at Oak Hill Country Club

Most of the people who follow golf would ponder at another moment at Oak Hill in 2013 that had more of an impact at this country club than the PGA Championship. Let me explain the circumstances.

It was a very grueling year for all the employees. The 95th PGA Championship had ended, and the club was ready to resume the year with some sort of normalcy. Right around Labor Day, (which was Monday, September 2), Ben Harmon, Craig's son who was majoring in music at some institution of higher learning in the Boston area and one of my honor caddies at that time, approached me with some news that not too many other people outside the immediate family were aware of.

"Joe," he said. "My father will be retiring from Oak Hill at the end of the year. You're one of the few individuals who will be informed before it gets to the press."

I did have some inkling as to what was to occur. The news was a mild surprise but not shocking. Craig Harmon had been the head golf professional at Oak Hill Country Club for over forty years. Not only was Mr. Harmon a living legend at Oak Hill, he *was* Oak Hill! In all its glory and charm, you could visualize this in him.

When speaking, writing, or whatever, Craig Harmon and Oak Hill were synonymous. Being a part of the number one golfing family in America and to claim him as one of their own was a great honor for Oak Hill Country Club.

I myself had a great admiration and respect for Mr. Harmon as a supervisor, family man, businessman, and, at the time, an elite member of *Golf Digest's* top twenty-five instructors in America. He allowed the people associated with him directly (the assistant pros, other golf shop personnel, the Caddie Master, manager, and assistant manager of the Golf Service Center) to consume their meals in the members' Grill Room (as opposed to the employees' dining area), where they could receive recognition from the members and their guests. It was not uncommon to see these select individuals having meals with the membership at the club. This privilege was discontinued when Mr. Harmon retired.

It was an absolute honor and special benefit to have been associated with Craig and his family. It was my personal belief that when Mr. Harmon decided to part ways with Oak Hill Country Club, Oak Hill lost a great piece of their history, prestige, and character.

So long, Mr. Craig Harmon; it was all my pleasure to truly know and work with/for you.

The Perks

A "perk," as explained in the Cambridge dictionary, is "an advantage or something extra such as, in money or goods, that you are given because of your job." As Caddie Master at Oak Hill Country Club, it came to be known that this was a benefit to which I was entitled. The perks came in many forms such as cash, mostly in bones (a term familiar in the golfing industry, referring to giving or throwing the dog a bone.) I got invitations to play golf around the world, including some of the most historic courses known to man; front row tickets to concerts, assorted sporting events, nightclub entertainment; dinners—you name it.

Just to mention a few of these bonuses, a member (D. M. M.) surprisingly picked up the total bill at a fine dining establishment in Rochester for my family and I. My daughter also worked at Oak Hill CC as a waitress, which probably contributed to this person's generosity.

Another gentleman (E. F.) who happened to own one of the largest automobile parts businesses in the Eastern US offered tickets to the Daytona 500 on a couple of different occasions and prime seating at Madison Square Garden for a National Hockey League (NHL) encounter featuring the New York Rangers hosting the

Washington Capitals; it was my personal option to select any game of my choice.

On yet another occasion, another member from Oak Hill CC (D. F.) was responsible for granting my party four tickets to witness a last-minute comeback from his alma mater (and my favorite NCAA football team at that time), the Syracuse Orange, over the University of South Florida at Raymond James Stadium in Tampa.

I also benefitted in acquiring premier seating at a Tim McGraw–Faith Hill concert, as well as an invitation to be present for comedian Ron White's engagement at a local club in the greater Rochester area.

I was the recipient of many bones as the Caddie Master at Oak Hill, but there was one that outshone all the others. I somewhat recollect I had mentioned earlier in this book that in the offseason, I was employed by several other golfing establishments in the state of Florida. A member from OHCC brought a contingent of fellow golfers from the TCC located in Tequesta, Florida, and they were also members of the Ridgewood CC in Paramus, New Jersey, as was the member (F. R.) himself.

Mr. E.T. and two other gentlemen (Mr. B. and Mr. D.) flew in to Oak Hill CC as the guests of Mr. F. R. for a friendly round of golf. As the three invited golfers assembled in their respective golf carts, Mr. E. T. summoned the Caddie Master over. As we exchanged our pleasant greetings to each other, Mr. E. T. extended his enclosed hand to me, holding a wad of bills.

"This little gift is from the boys at Turtle Creek in appreciation for all you do for us."

God, I figured, *there must be one hundred dollars here.* Much to my surprise, when I returned back to the caddie area, I opened my fist to discover five one hundred-dollar bills! And to top it off, the member (Mr. F. R.) exited the clubhouse and returned to his entourage waiting to tee off on the first hole of the Championship Course. But before that occurred, he called me over.

"Thanks, Joe," he said and slipped me another Ben Franklin!

I responded, "Thank you, Mr. R., and your guests for your utmost generosity."

Needless to mention, that incident didn't happen again.

It is now time to mention the over three hundred golf invitations I received from members and guests alike to play golf at some of the finest and most historic courses and country clubs in the world. These included Oakmont; Winged Foot; Pine Valley; the Players' Championship Course in Jacksonville, Florida; the Medalist; Riviera (California); Old Head (Ireland), the Old Course at St. Andrew's (Scotland), Hong Kong (PRC), Royale Melbourne (Australia), and—how could I forget—Augusta National. A couple of these also included air flight and hotel accommodations for my wife and me! Unfortunately, because of my responsibility to my job, family matters, time for travel, and other commitments, I was unable to take advantage of any of these opportunities.

Perhaps the greatest gift that was bestowed upon the Caddie Master occurred when a philanthropic, generous member (R. P.) gave a close relative of mine diagnosed with a rare blood cancer the red carpet treatment at his center, which was part of the University of Rochester Medical System. Before arriving at the cancer center, my relative was given a maximum of seven years to survive. That was in 2016. She was later informed by her specialist (who happened to have treated said member's father) that if she indeed passed away before that time, cancer would not be the culprit. We are now in the year 2024. Do the math. Was the cure a result of medical science or divine intervention? Whatever the reason, no one can put a price on the outcome. My sincerest gratitude to this wonderful member and philanthropist.

THE LAST DAYS

My Final Year

2013 had been a physically and mentally draining year. The wet weather combined with another Major at the club had dramatic effects on the caddie program. The sheer number of corporate events (outings) coupled with more than generous guest lists contributed to the demand being higher than the supply of caddies on many days. On most of the busiest days, it was not uncommon to have caddies go out twice and, on some rare occasions, even three times on a particular day. In fact, I had one caddie on my roster, D. M., who singled, forecaddied, doubled, and singled again in one twenty-four-hour period. (I had neglected at first to give a spot in the program because of the limited number of new caddies I selected, but he eventually became a fine caddie and a very respectful lad.)

My suffering was due solely to the no-cart rulings, which happened more times than I wish to remember. Depleting the supply of caddies on any given day was not uncommon. Free push carts supplied by the club (to benefit those who would rather walk than ride) was beneficial in that season, but at the expense of the caddie program every other year. I had more complaints in 2013 than all the other years combined (mainly during the Men's Invitational, which, of course, was without riding golf carts). It came down to basic economics of supply and demand and, believe it or not, man's inability to control the weather.

Oak Hill CC (Post-2013)

When Craig Harmon retired at the end of the 2013 golf season, my beloved Oak Hill CC changed dramatically. The board of directors decided to go with younger blood with no head golf professional experience at all. It appeared to me the new philosophy was that the pro shop would be responsible for operating all phases of the Golf Service Center and not the manager of the outside operations, who had seventeen years of knowledge and experience at that position.

Everything changed; even a new general manager was recruited. It appeared to me that both the new head pro and the general manager must have had extremely impressive résumés, reason being that this was Oak Hill and not just another ordinary private country club!

Eventually, all the changes that were being implemented forced many of the older workers out, either by their own choosing or the illogical decisions of the new management, and I am specifically talking about older employees with careers. It was apparent that the new_management at Oak Hill CC, both the golfing and the food and beverage divisions, wanted a new look at the club. They replaced seasoned employees with "kids," relatives, friends, and whoever else it benefited them to hire (politics), not realizing all the experience they had terminated.

I have been around for many years, and one just cannot offer quality workmanship when most of the workers are young with no or very limited background in the service industry.

Some of the new hires were appointed as interns to work in the pro shop and for the Golf Service Center. They were given free room at a luxury apartment building located not far from the club and a guaranteed forty-hour workweek. These interns were attempting to acquire their cards, completing a course designed by the PGA. Once they attained this card, they would join an elite group of about thirty thousand other cardholders of the PGA. Many of these "pros" figured one day they would be teeing it up on the PGA Tour or be the Head Golf Professional or Director of Golf at a country club, preferably a private one. Obviously, very few would accomplish this feat, and many would become despondent with the probability of having to search for a career outside the golf industry and in the real world.

Post-2013

Personal observation and feedback from other workers, caddies, and members confirmed that the quality of service had diminished and the atmosphere that we once enjoyed in Oak Hill CC in the pre-2014 era had disappeared. The "new" Oak Hill was a far cry from the manner in which the club had operated in the past, and it was definitely not for the better (but hopefully this has changed since said period). The general manager who had been there for twenty-four years was forced to resign in late 2012 due to political pressure, and the following two general managers were no match.

New Players

It was 2014. Mr. Harmon had relocated to Florida, and the general manager's contract was not renewed. Therefore, two new players entered the arena. A new head professional (NHP) and a new general manager (NGM) were chosen over hundreds of applicants. The NHP had been on the staff at some exclusive country clubs but was never a head professional at any of them. The NGM had held that position at some finer clubs and resorts but was also a person with local connections. I heard there were some politics involved in at least one (if not both) of the selections; I even recall that a fellow employee in the know informed me that someone who filled one of the positions was not the first choice. I could be wrong, but I am only reporting what could be the case. Both appointees were much younger than their predecessors, and they were determined to make Oak Hill CC better. Not from my perspective, but you couldn't just replace a Harmon nor a Ruler either as far as I was concerned.

First of all, it appeared both new employees had a problem with other experienced employees over the age of forty. Every department was involved except accounting. It seemed every week that older, well-seasoned employees were terminated with little or, in most cases, no legitimate basis at all. Some had decided to leave on their own, the reason being the NHP and NGM created an atmosphere that was difficult for them to remain in.

I remember when Dyxmit suggested that I get into his Cub Car. He said, "We're going for a ride."

A man who was in command of the Golf Service Center, seventeen years behind the wheel, would have his responsibilities stripped from him, thus resulting in him being no more than a glorified bag boy. It appeared the NHP wanted his group of kids in the golf shop (no longer the pro shop) to run the show. What a joke, to say the least. Dyxmit mentioned to me, in total frustration, he just couldn't take it anymore. This new recruit (NHP), half Mr. Dyxmit's age, was unveiling how procedures would be accomplished in the future. In reality, things were progressively going downhill.

Communication—New Regime

Under the traditional staff (Harmon and the former general managers), communication was never a problem. A staff worker under their leadership always felt they were a valuable contribution to their team. And the ex-GM, Mr. D. F., who succeeded the Ruler, always kept the Caddie Master informed of the changes and ongoing circumstances at Oak Hill Country Club and in the golf world; it was not quite so with the new regime. Case in point—in the summer of the previous year, the then acting GM had notified me that there would be a newsworthy meeting to be held at the Congressional Country Club in Bethesda, Maryland, to discuss the possibility of establishing a Ryder Cup Tournament for the Champions Tour. The premier would be hosted by the Congressional, scheduled to be in 2015. The first on European soil would follow in 2016, and on the return trip to the United States, the next stop would be at Oak Hill Country Club in 2017. The exact forecasting of this event was yet to be made, but it was mentioned in several golf publications.

So the NHP approached me one day to inform me that he would be absent for a few days as he headed to the Congressional Country Club. I humbly asked him if the Champions Ryder Cup was still in the discussion stage.

He appeared shocked. "Where did you hear about that?" he questioned.

"Oh, I've been in the loop for about a year now. I first heard it from D. F., and since then my friend and coworker the TV has been filling me in," I responded.

NHP acted like a top military secret had been exposed. The TV was the head maintenance personnel at Oak Hill. If you wanted to know anything about anything or the latest gossip, you talked to the TV. The new regime eventually terminated his career at the club, probably due to his age combined with the fact that he possessed more knowledge about the club than anyone else.

Eventually, the Champions Tour Ryder Cup fizzled. I believe it would not have been financially lucrative for the television networks. Besides, it was too immense of a gamble to pursue and there were too many obstacles to overcome.

The multitude of employees who were responsible for making Oak Hill the number one country club in the country just five years previously were being terminated, in most cases solely because of their age. Let's get it straight—it's age discrimination no matter how you look at it. It happens at many country clubs; they don't need any reason to fire anyone. Of the four private clubs where I had been employed, every one contained a provision stating so. Age discrimination is rampant in corporate America; in fact, it happens in every area of life! Not only did these employees suffer the loss of their livelihood, the NGM used it to negate paying end-of-year bonuses to the Caddie Master and other deserving staff members, who had completed a full season of service to the membership and others. The unreasonable lack of common-sense excuse provided by the NGM was the personnel involved were not on the payroll when the bonuses were distributed.

After an extremely long and busy season, and with the new players on board, Oak Hill Country Club definitely was not the same country club it had been for years. Whereas in the past you could access membership if you were sponsored, in good standing, and could pay the one-time initiation fee, it was now possible to stretch this over a period of four years. Let's say initiation was one-time sixty-thousand-dollar expense, now one could pay fifteen thousand a year for four years. Many people receive that plus more on Social Security! In actuality, the class of the membership was watered down. What was a highly white-collar club in the past was transforming into a somewhat blue-collar club. That occurred at many private clubs across the country, in most cases just so they could stay above water. I had caddies who became members! The quality of the club and the membership had changed drastically. Many members decided to quit and relocated their memberships elsewhere.

Many employees (such as the Caddie Master) found work elsewhere and voluntarily departed. Unfortunately, this was not the case for most. It left a void in my life at the club to witness such disrespect aimed at my friends and fellow workers by those in power responsible driving these people out of the labor force solely based on their age. I had a good number of honor caddies, some over forty and many very close to that age. My one big question is why didn't management terminate these independent contractors? Surprisingly, those in power would eventually almost double the rates, which I had unsuccessfully attempted to do for years!

The Case of the Missing Putter

Back in the summer of 2014 (the year I had decided would be my last at Oak Hill CC), I had texted one of my honor caddies, Carney, on that Sunday afternoon to inquire if he could possibly caddy double for a member and his guest in a couple of hours. He gave me his affirmation, and he arrived about an hour later.

After the round had been completed, Carney, as was customary, checked the bags for a final time before placing the clubs in the golf back rack located in the bag drop area. For some reason, when the twosome arrived to take their respective belongings home, the guest discovered that his brand-new Titleist Scotty Cameron putter was missing (worth three hundred dollars). As would be expected, the golfer proceeded to the pro shop to inform the staff of the situation.

Out of nowhere, I was bombarded with accusations from Jersey Jeff of the New Head Pro's' (NHP) staff that Carney had stolen the property! The caddie vehemently denied the allegations for the missing property when I confronted him. Jersey continued yelling his choice words at the Caddie Master, expecting him to make the Scotty Cameron appear. There was no proof at all, just assumptions. There were many people passing through the bag drop area, including his outside staff who were not paid anything close to a caddie's wage. What was this individual's problem? If he truly suspected the caddie (which I did not), why didn't he pursue the matter? He was just convinced that since Carney was the caddie and there was a putter missing, that the caddie was responsible for the crime. I could not believe I was being addressed by Jersey Jeff in this manner. He and the Caddie Master had enjoyed a very good relationship up to this time, or so I had believed. We had nothing even close to this under Harmon's reign. Oh well. I soon departed from the club after that incident. I never received an explanation nor a conclusion (or an apology, which I never expected anyway).

A Change in Life

With the new management also came the feeling and reality of no longer being an integral part of the golfing experience of members, guests, and celebrities at this great institution. The respect for people who dedicated significant parts of their lives to make Oak Hill CC such a distinguished place was forgotten and eventually non-existent. I personally could no longer please everyone; you name it—members, guests, administration, caddies, whoever. I dug myself a hole trying to be Mr. Nice Guy, but it came to a point where being employed at Oak Hill CC was no longer possible. I finally left my beloved Oak Hill on my own terms and conditions and relocated permanently to my new place of employment at another platinum private club on Sanibel Island, Florida. What a great move! And I didn't believe anywhere could be better than working at a fine, distinguished, and prestigious country club as Oak Hill. What a pleasant surprise.

Tidbits

For those at Oak Hill CC who had thought that I had passed on, I am still kicking and have many fond memories of my years at this elite country club, both as a teenager and as an adult. It was a great way to end my career and to retire in paradise. Also, I obtained a great, worthy learning experience, mostly in thanksgiving to the younger generation. Just to mention a few tidbits on the list:

- There is no longer any privacy in the world. Once you have done anything via the cell phone or computer, you become prey for anyone.
- I spent at least thirty percent, if not more, of my time as Caddie Master on my cell phone, usually attempting to contact caddies who were too lazy to arrive early in the morning. On top of that, on many occasions, members requested caddies at the last minute. I eventually discovered (and it didn't take long) that caddies were reluctant to verbally communicate, but they will always respond via text.
- If a caddie misses an assignment, they receive one warning and then dismissal on the second occurrence. I'm positive my reputation was tarnished by hanging on to certain individuals I should have terminated on several occasions. A prime example—it was a practice of mine to pair caddies

with golfers (mostly members) of similar backgrounds. I accepted a kid from an ex-assistant pro who landed the head professional position at another private club in the vicinity. He was giving this adolescent a break, and he knew I would assist him in this situation. So this high school student had been on my roster for about a year, just an average A caddie. The member for whom he would forecaddie happened to be an alumnus at the same institution the lad was attending. A perfect match one would think, right? The round came to completion, and the member and his guest returned to the caddie area.

"Joe, the worst caddie I have ever had here," he fumed. He had paid the kid the minimum and stated that was too generous. The caddie stated that he was tired. Most likely hung over. And this was a two o'clock in the afternoon tee time! Luckily, it was late in the year, and I never saw the caddie again. Trying to do the head pro a favor turned disastrous—not good for Mr. Nice Guy. It was my understanding that just after this incident, said head pro was terminated for…let's say conduct detrimental to his respective country club.

I tried to satisfy everyone, members, guests, and caddies. I admit I was too soft on my boys. Another example. This teacher (an honor caddie) happened to accept an offer from a member, a super nice guy, but he didn't compensate his caddies well, and the caddie knew it. It was in 2013 when caddies were at a premium for the Men's Invitational. Instead of the caddie honoring his commitment, he approached me and pleaded that I assign him to someone who paid better. Why did I allow this caddie to make his problem my problem? Unfortunately, I complied. Never should have done it. Not only did I tick off the member, but I never did forgive myself for putting a caddie's mistake before the member's request.

- Caddies need to think before they speak. Dozens of times in my career, I asked caddies if they could loop at, say, ten o'clock tomorrow. And they would reply, "In the morning?" Think about it.

- Many good caddies should join AA, no matter at what private club they are employed.
- Many poor performing caddies should do likewise. Better yet, find another job!
- Caddying is a fantastic method of finding a great full-time career in any field.
- Caddies who bitched about their pay usually deserved what they received.
- In the golf business, always have the member satisfaction as your number one priority, regardless of where you are located.
- I had a caddie in my program named Lenny who suffered from AHDD, according to his friend and fellow caddie, J. D. Lenny was a decent caddie, but I would say he was a bogey golfer in his own right. It kind of struck me and a few other caddies who were present at the time when he seriously mentioned that there was a flaw in Tiger Woods's swing.
- In all my years at Oak Hill CC, that is, from 2002–2014, I only had the opportunity to play a round of golf on either course more than about a half dozen times. I lived thirty-seven miles from the club, and I would either have to work as Caddie Master for an outing of some sort or the club would have guest day activities starting at 2:00 p.m. Whatever the case, it would be my responsibility to have caddies available to serve the members and/or guests. And because of the lack of practice, my golf game suffered, and it was not worth the aggravation and frustration to travel that distance.
- There was a time (I believe it was 2008, the year of the 69th Senior PGA Championship) that I did work 109 days straight. Only in the private sector is this possible...

It is my personal belief (throughout my career at Oak Hill) that said country club is desperately attempting to get in bed with the USGA for the sole purpose of hosting their fourth US Open (as in 1956, 1968, and 1989), much like the Merion Golf Club outside of Philadelphia had the honor of doing so in 2013 and will again repeat as host in this prestigious tournament in 2030. In their last US Open, the yardage for the championship was listed as seven thousand yards, which in reality was 6,997, as I was informed by a member of both establishments. I guess that seven thousand is the magic number. What was a blessing in this case was the fact that the event took the driver, four wedges, and a putter game plan out of the players' habitual round and forced them to use just about every other club in their arsenal. I wish Oak Hill the best of luck with their attempt in procuring this tournament; they deserve it, but my belief is that it will never happen. Sure, Oak Hill could shorten the course significantly to Merion's distance, but there is little room for extending. However, due to its overall acreage, it would not be able to accommodate the number of patrons to which a championship of this magnitude is entitled. It is a great course on which to caddy since the distance from green to tee is so short. But six-story pavilions are not the solution, as were present in the 2023 PGA Championship.

Retiring from Oak Hill Country Club

I had known in early August of 2014 that I would not be back at my Caddie Master position the following season due to the fact that I had accepted a position at the Sanctuary Golf Club on Sanibel Island in Florida and had committed myself to the following June of 2015. Therefore, I would be staying in sunny, somewhat tropical Florida and not rushing back to the cold, snowy, wet, and dreary weather of Upstate New York in early April as I had done in the previous twelve years. What a relief!

Although I had enjoyed my career at Oak Hill CC (and I still miss it), I wholeheartedly believed it was time to retire and move forward. The decision to leave Oak Hill CC was mine and mine alone, even though management would dishonestly have you believe otherwise.

Conclusion

In conclusion, I find it necessary to extend my apologies to any person, regardless of their role at the club, who feels offended by what I have written or done as the Caddie Master. There was no intent to downgrade or dissatisfy anyone. I am grateful to Oak Hill Country Club, the members, fellow employees, the head professionals, the caddies, pro shop staff, the general managers, and guests for all the friendships I was able to muster. I also regret the friendships I surrendered because of misunderstandings and failures in communication, be it my personal fault or the other parties involved. I was truly blessed to be given the opportunity to work and to serve the people at such a great historical and prestigious country club as Oak Hill.

Believe it or not, I totally enjoyed my time as the Caddie Master at Oak Hill Country Club. It was a fantastic and rewarding career, but never did I realize how much of a celebrity status that position held in the golf world until I retired from this marvelous establishment. So be it. I made many lasting friendships at the club with fellow workers, members, professional golfers, celebrities, guests, and, of course, caddies. I have been away from this particular location for quite some time now. I apologize to all those I left a negative impact on at Oak Hill CC and in the caddie program. I am ever thankful to Oak Hill and its membership for allowing me to serve them in my capacity for thirteen years. I still have thoughts of Oak Hill CC just about daily, and it will possess a special place in my heart forever.

Figure 13: Back side of Oak Hill clubhouse.

About The Author

The author was the Caddie Master at Oak Hill Country Club in Rochester, NY from 2002-2014, which was where he was born and raised. Prior to that, he graduated with a B.S. in Industrial Relations from a small college in upstate NY, and eventually started a career at Eastman Kodak Company for 27 years. I relocated to SW FL permanently in 2016, Married to my wife Beverly for forty plus years and have a son Aaron (PhD economics) and daughter Rachel Meisenzahl (Financial Advisor). Enjoy golf, travel, reading and following the five grandchildren, age 5-16, two involved on the UnderArmour SWFL Jr. PGA Tour; two others in year-round ice hockey; and my granddaughter participating in Top Dog, a national cheer organization. Life is good.

$\mathcal{A}$CKNOWLEDGMENTS

There are many human factors involved in the compilation of a book that need to be mentioned, especially as a sign of gratitude that made it possible. First of all, I would like to thank my family and friends for their patience and input in any form. It has taken the author nine years to complete this work, mainly due to the lack of computer skills and what procedures need to be taken to attain my goal. I haven't used a computer in any regularity since being laid off from Eastman Kodak Co. shortly after the terrorist attack of 9/11/01, and was never offered one for my position as Caddie Master at Oak Hill Country Club. First of all, every detail was done "old school". I began writing scratch in notebooks on a variety of topics. After writing down everything that only I could read, I then re-wrote in well-structured cursive penmanship. Astonishingly, when I presented my 14 year-old, 155 IQ grandson to type it, he stated he could not because he was never taught cursive writing in the public school system due to the fact that educators (?) no longer recognized it as being beneficial. What a joke! It resulted in the typing responsibilities to be split between my son and I. Being my only attempt in writing a book, it was truly a great learning experience.

I would also like to mention a word of gratitude to Craig Harmon, General Managers Eric Rule (presently at Kinloch C.C.) and

Dan Farrell (may he RIP), and especially Dyxmit, (Dick Schmidt), who contributed to making my position at Oak Hill C.C. as comfortable as possible.

Loads of thanks must be showered upon all the caddies, many of whom I have mentioned in this book, who just by their mannerisms contributed greatly to the creation of this work of non-fiction.

I am humbly thankful to the multitude of celebrities, athletes, PGA Tour professionals, fellow employees, and especially the members of Oak Hill C.C and their guests who participated in making my position as Caddie Master enjoyable and a pleasure to have served them all.

A personal sign of gratitude to the several guests who found the time and effort to write letters of appreciation for the hospitality I provided for them on behalf of Oak Hill C.C.

But none of this would be possible at all without the love and support of my wife Beverly and my children Aaron (PhD) (Lindsay;) and Rachel Meisenzahl (Karl). And let's not forget the grandkids – Aaron's (Evan, Brynlee and Jack) and Rachel's (Calvin and Charlie Meisenzahl) during this most trying time.

A very special thank you to my son Aaron for surrendering all his time and energy in assisting me with his bountiful knowledge of the computer and its applications and his constant communication with me. Had it not been for his help, this book may have taken another few years.

And let's not forget thanking the Lord and St. Anthony (Turn Around Tony) for the divine assistance for finding a way for the completion of this document.